GENERATIONS

OTHER BOOKS BY MCKADE MARSHALL

Tasting the Goodness of God

Breathe

Finding Your Keys

Why I Stand with Israel

GENERATIONS

McKade Marshall

"His truth endures to all generations…"
Psalm 100:5

I dedicate this book to my parents, grandparents, and family.
May God bless our family lines greatly for generations to come.

Copyright © 2026 by McKade Marshall

MLM Publishing
PO Box 533
Malibu, CA 90265
www.mckademarshall.com

All rights reserved. In accordance with the U.S. Copyright Act of 1976, the scanning, uploading, and electronic sharing of any part of this book without permission of the publisher is unlawful piracy and theft of the author's intellectual property. If you would like to use material from the book (other than for review purposes), prior written permission must be obtained by contacting the publisher. Thank you for your support of the author's rights.

Scripture quotations marked (ESV) are from the The Holy Bible, English Standard Version® (ESV®), copyright © 2001 by Crossway, a publishing ministry of Good News Publishers. Used by permission. All rights reserved.

Scripture quotations marked (NASB/NASB95) are taken from the New American Standard Bible®, Copyright © 1960, 1962, 1963, 1968, 1971, 1972, 1973, 1975, 1977, 1995 by The Lockman Foundation. Used by permission. (www.lockman.org)

Scripture quotations marked (NCV) are taken from the New Century Version. Copyright © 2005 by Thomas Nelson, Inc. Used by permission. All rights reserved.

Scripture quotations marked (NIV) are taken from the Holy Bible, New International Version®, NIV®. Copyright © 1973, 1978, 1984, 2011 by Biblica, Inc.™ Used by permission of Zondervan. All rights reserved worldwide. www.zondervan.com The "NIV" and "New International Version" are trademarks registered in the United States Patent and Trademark Office by Biblica, Inc.™

Scripture quotations marked (NKJV) are taken from the New King James Version®. Copyright © 1982 by Thomas Nelson, Inc. Used by permission. All rights reserved.

Scripture quotations marked (NLT) are taken from the Holy Bible, New Living Translation, Copyright © 1996, 2004, 2007, 2013 by Tyndale House Foundation. Used by permission of Tyndale House Publishers, Inc., Carol Stream, Illinois 60188. All rights reserved.

Scripture taken from the Berean Study Bible (BSB), used by permission from the Berean Foundation.

Scripture taken from The Holy Bible, Berean Literal Bible, BLB. Public Domain.

Interior design by Miles McFarland.

Library of Congress Control Number: 2026932184
ISBN: 979-8-218-91235-2

Printed in the United States of America

TABLE OF CONTENTS

Introduction   9

PART ONE: SPEAK

Chapter One	Breaking Generational Curses	15
Chapter Two	Declaring Generational Blessings	25
Chapter Three	How to Prophesy	35
Chapter Four	Leadership	45
Chapter Five	Servanthood	55

PART TWO: BELIEVE

Chapter Six	Passing the Mantle	67
Chapter Seven	Spirit of Unbelief	77
Chapter Eight	Dreamers Like Joseph	87
Chapter Nine	Breaking Barriers	97
Chapter Ten	Vision of the Black Mantle	107

PART THREE: CREATE

Chapter Eleven	Starting Over	119
Chapter Twelve	Your Prayer Life	129
Chapter Thirteen	4:44	139
Chapter Fourteen	Having a Wealthy Mind	149
Chapter Fifteen	Thinking in Color	159

PART FOUR: DEVOTE

Chapter Sixteen	Having a History with God	171
Chapter Seventeen	God Revealed Throughout Time	181
Chapter Eighteen	Psalm 78	191
Chapter Nineteen	Staying in Faith	201
Chapter Twenty	Leaving a Legacy	211

Conclusion	221

INTRODUCTION

Faith is handed down from one generation to the next. The Hebrew word for "generations" is Toldot. Toldot can also be translated as "descendants". With each generation, a line of descendants is formed. The decisions made from one generation can release a blessing or a curse on the generation that follows. We see this throughout the Scriptures. In the weekly Torah portion readings in the Jewish cycle, Toldot is the sixth weekly reading, which usually falls sometime in November. On this week, Toldot (or "generations") covers the story of Jacob and Esau, Isaac's twin boys.

The conflict between these two sons of Isaac has carried ramifications for centuries. The faith of Jacob and the lack thereof in Esau can be used allegorically to compare the flesh versus the Spirit, which is the internal struggle we all must endure as we seek to follow Christ. Jacob greatly desired the father's blessing. Esau took the inherited blessing as the firstborn son for granted. The outcome was that the descendants of Jacob became the blessed lineage that would one day give us the birth of Israel's Messiah, Jesus.

Because Jacob fought for the blessing unabated, generational blessings were released over his "toldot", the Hebrew people. Jacob worked for twenty years to have the woman of his dreams (Rachel). He wrestled an angel all night until daybreak at the ford of the Jabbok until God blessed him (Genesis 32:22-31). The relentless faith seen in Jacob is the faith we should all strive to have for our own family lines. I believe Jacob knew the power of the family bloodline, so he was willing to do whatever it takes to ensure the future of his family would be blessed greatly.

In the same way, we have a decision to make today that will determine the fate of the next generation tomorrow. The result of Jacob's decisions was twelve Hebrew tribes: a tiny, but powerful, nation of Jewish people. Four thousand years later, we are still eating the good fruit of Jacob's decision to wrestle for the blessing and follow after his God. We are all under the divine care of God the Father. Just as the Father took care of Jacob and his family through every battle, He is going to take care of you and your loved ones.

The reason God continually blessed Jacob is that he mixed his faith with action. Likewise, we must take action based on our faith. When I structured this book, I separated it into four sections: Speak, Believe, Create, and Devote. When we speak the word of God over our lives, power is released for the Spirit to go to work. When we believe in God's Word and His promises, our faith in Christ causes mountains to come down. As human beings created in the image of God, we have His divine attributes dwelling in us. Just as He is Creator of all things, so we have the ability to create and do great works for God and His Kingdom. Lastly, when we choose to devote our hearts to the Lord, we are establishing blessings that will carry on, even after we leave this world.

At the end of each chapter, I have written questions to answer. These questions are to provoke deeper thought about what you have just read and to help you apply what you are learning. Also, at the end of each chapter are Scripture readings. I have chosen two passages from the Old Testament and two from the New Testament. These Scriptures provide Biblical truths that can help us build our lives in a way that is pleasing to the Lord. The Apostle Paul says in 2 Timothy 3:16-17 (NIV), "All Scripture is God-breathed and is useful for teaching, rebuking, correcting and training in righteousness, so that the servant of God may be thoroughly equipped for every good work."

When God hovered over the waters of the earth on the first day of creation, He had not spoken anything into existence. Genesis 1:2 says the world began formless and void, nothing but ocean and darkness. The waters may have looked something like the cover of this book. When Noah floated on the ark with his family and the animal kingdom for an entire year, he experienced a redo of God's creation. Just as the world was coverd in nothing but water at the beginning of time, so the great flood of Noah brought about a global baptism covering the whole earth again.

The world before the flood looked much different than what it does today. A new world was established with Noah, his wife, and his three sons and their wives. In the same way, when we come to know Jesus Christ, the old self is washed away. Just as God flooded the earth (a baptism) because it was corrupt and violent, so we are baptized into Jesus Christ. Ephesians 4:22 (NLT) says to "throw off your old sinful nature and your former way of life, which is corrupted by lust and deception." We must come to Jesus if we are to be washed of our sins.

At the end of this era, there will be one final baptism. This baptism will be one of fire, one that will destroy the heavens and the earth as we know them. This world and its creation will be replaced with a new, incorruptible one. 2 Peter 3:13 (NLT) tells us, "But we are looking forward to the new heavens and new earth He has promised, a world filled with God's righteousness." Once again, the symbolism of the heavens and the earth is found in the gospel. John the Baptist says in Matthew 3:11 (NLT), "I baptize with water those who repent of their sins and turn to God. But someone is coming soon who is greater than I am—so much greater that I'm not worthy even to be His slave and carry His sandals. He will baptize you with the Holy Spirit and with fire."

When we come to Jesus, we are baptized in water as a public profession of our faith in Christ. In Jesus' name, we are also baptized in the fire of the Holy Spirit. The earth underwent a water baptism, and a new earth was filled with Noah's descendants. The Son of God came and died on the Cross to take away the sins of the world. In judgment, God will baptize the earth with fire. Those who are born again in Christ will inherit a new, everlasting heaven and earth. God has revealed these deep mysteries of His divine plan of redemption throughout history and throughout His Word.

With each passing generation, God is revealing Himself. I pray the Lord reveals more of Himself to you in a personal way as you read each chapter of this book. I encourage you to read this book with a friend, spouse, or prayer group. The questions and Scriptures at the end of each chapter are great learning tools to help you grow in your faith and experience more of God's goodness in your life. I believe because you've chosen to pick up this book and read it, God is going to pour out more of His abundant favor and blessings on you and your loved ones. He is going to release His angels into your life in a special way, and you are going to see real change that is going to last for generations to come in Jesus' name.

Part One

SPEAK

"Whoever speaks is to do so as one who is speaking actual words of God…"
1 Peter 4:11

Chapter One
BREAKING GENERATIONAL CURSES

When God spoke almost 6,000 years ago, the power of His words created the universe and the beginning of time. The power of His eternal words brought into existence all that we now see, hear, touch, smell, and taste. Six days into the divine Creator speaking into existence all living things in the universe He said, "Let Us make mankind in Our image, in Our likeness, so that they may rule over the fish in the sea and the birds in the sky, over the livestock and all the wild animals, and over all the creatures that move along the ground." (Genesis 1:26 NIV)

When God created Adam, forming him from the dust of the ground, He breathed into him the breath of life. Adam was unlike anything God had created on the earth or throughout any of the universe's billions of galaxies. Adam was made by the direct hand of the Living God. Adam had God's air in his lungs. Adam was made in the very image of his omnipotent Creator. Adam was set apart from all living things in order to rule over God's magnificent creation.

Adam was flawless and perfect in every way. However, we all know the story. Adam and Eve are enticed by the serpent, who is the devil, and eat the forbidden fruit. The first sin of man led to the first curses invoked by God for their disobedience. Eve is cursed with severe childbearing and submission to her husband. Adam is cursed with painful toil in order to eat from the ground that is also now cursed. Furthermore, mankind was cursed with the final sentence of eventual death. God tells Adam in Genesis 3:19 (NLT), "By the sweat of your brow will you have food to eat until you return to the ground from which you were made. For you were made from dust, and to dust you will return."

Friends, curses are a very real thing. When we violate something God says, we are invoking a curse. Our words and our actions always come with a consequence, whether good or bad. Furthermore, if the words and actions that are not in alignment with God's Word are not corrected, they can cause us problems our entire life. The mindset we are indoctrinated with and carry from birth must be transformed into the mindset of Jesus Christ, the Son of God, if we are going to experience a life of freedom that God intended for us to have.

The thinking that "grandpa did it, grandma did it, momma and daddy did it, so I do it" can be a snare if the habit is not a Biblical or healthy habit. This is why we must continually examine ourselves. Lamentations 3:40 (NIV) tells us, "Let us examine our ways and test them, and let us return to the Lord." Inheritance, legacy, and family traditions are something we are all born into. These things - like money, habits, genetic predispositions, and family history - are bestowed upon us at birth.

We all were born into different types of families and traditions. Some of us are born into unfair situations, while others are born into privileges unearned. Exodus 34:6-7 (NLT) says, "The LORD passed in front of Moses, calling out, 'Yahweh! The LORD! The God of compassion and mercy! I am slow to anger and filled with unfailing love and faithfulness. I lavish unfailing love to a thousand generations. I forgive iniquity, rebellion, and sin. But I do not excuse the guilty. I lay the sins of the parents upon their children and grandchildren; the entire family is affected— even children in the third and fourth generations.'"

When we or someone in our generational line sins, there is a repercussion in the family line. This sin passes from one generation to the next if not dealt with. This is why it is so important that we learn how to break generational curses that could be plaguing us and keeping us from having a better life. The only way to break generational curses is through Jesus Christ. Jesus is the curse breaker. He is the only one who can permanently break a generational curse.

The Apostle Paul tells the early church in Galatians 3:13 (NKJV), "Christ has redeemed us from the curse of the law, having become a curse for us (for it is written, 'Cursed is everyone who hangs on a tree')." When Jesus was crucified to the cross, He was cursed by God for our sins. He took generational curses on His body when He was beaten, bruised, and torn. The wrath that we deserved for our sins fell upon Him. He is the only man that can wash away generational curses completely.

Apart from Christ's sacrifice there is no atonement for sin. Doing good works, reading self-help books, and forming better habits alone will not wash away sin. While these things can be helpful for having a better life, they do not cover sin. The blood of Jesus is the only thing powerful enough to remove sin indefinitely. The Apostle John tells us in 1 John 1:7 (NLT), "But if we are living in the light, as God is in the light, then we have fellowship with each other, and the blood of Jesus, His Son, cleanses us from all sin."

Step one to removing generational curses is first bringing the sin, or the curse, to the light. When we acknowledge that there is a problem, we know what we need to pray for specifically. For example, in my family line there is substance abuse, immorality, squandering of wealth, and other sins that have come down the generational tree. In order for me to deal with these generational curses that I have spent much of my life battling against, I must first acknowledge that this is an issue in my family lineage.

The next step is to repent of these sins, repent on behalf of my relatives who have gone before me, and repent of any of these sins I have participated in myself. When we confess and repent of generational sins, God promises to forgive us. The Apostle John goes on to say in 1 John 1:9 (NIV), "If we confess our sins, He is faithful and just and will forgive us our sins and purify us from all unrighteousness." Confession of sin is the key that unlocks any strongholds the devil has on us.

When we confess our sins to God, His Spirit goes to work cleansing our conscience and our mind. In that very instant you are forgiven. There is no need to keep asking for forgiveness. Ask for forgiveness, receive God's mercy, and move forward in faith. One common mistake I see within the church is people who confess their sin, try to move forward, but then the enemy wants to keep bringing it up. The devil wants to keep us chained to sins we no longer are bound to. Those sins were nailed to the cross and forgiven. Even others, who may not necessarily have impure motives, may want you to keep bringing up past sins. They want to hear far too many details of the testimony, if you will. I call this beating a dead horse.

Recalling the deeds of darkness committed in the past does not please the Lord. Ephesians 5:12 (NLT) says, "It is shameful even to talk about the things that ungodly people do in secret." Brothers and sisters, if anyone - even a Christian counselor or pastor - tries to pump you for information that you have already been forgiven of, this is not of God. If God forgave you, you are forgiven. Reliving past mistakes and failures is not the path to freedom, and any ministry or church that teaches otherwise is not helping you. On the contrary, they are crippling you and causing unnecessary pain.

The Apostle Paul, who murdered the first Christian believers, had to learn to let go of the past. He had to learn to not let the devil keep him bound to his great sin. Paul says in Philippians 3:13 (NLT), "I focus on this one thing: Forgetting the past and looking forward to what lies ahead." Walking with God is like driving a car. If you are constantly looking out the rear view mirror, you are missing the entire front windshield with the view of where you are going. Like driving a car down the freeway, in our walks with God we are always moving forward.

If we are constantly looking back, we just might get into a traffic accident from not paying attention to what is in front of us! The same is true in your spiritual journey. If you are constantly looking back at the past, you are going to miss the opportunities right in front of you. You may even get into a spiritual accident from dwelling on the past. Throughout my life, I have seen too many people who are bound and even trapped by their past. Their thinking has become ensnared by history. Instead of looking ahead, grabbing hold of a new vision and what God wants to do, they dwell in the past. The future only repeats the past because of wrong thinking. The cycle must be broken by looking forward to new things.

The cost of following Jesus is the blessing of true freedom. The cost of following Jesus is the blessing of breaking free of generational curses. Jesus talks about this cost, and it puts his listeners to the test. Luke 9:61-62 (NLT) tells us, "Another said, 'Yes, Lord, I will follow You, but first let me say good-bye to my family.' But Jesus told him, 'Anyone who puts a hand to the plow and then looks back is not fit for the Kingdom of God.'" Sometimes we don't need to ask for the family's permission before we stop participating in certain activities we know violate God's Word. Choosing faith in Jesus over walking in family curses is a crossroad we all come to at some point in our lives.

Will I drink and party with the rest of the family on the weekends, or will I go to church and pursue righteous living (1 Peter 4:3)? Will I sleep with whomever I feel like sleeping with, live with whomever I so choose even out of wedlock because that's what my family does and permits, or will I rise above and choose to keep the marriage bed pure (Hebrews

13:4)? Will I roll out of bed on Sunday morning and attend church service even though no one else in my family does (Hebrews 10:25)? These are all questions that should enter our minds as we seek to break free of generational curses.

For some of us, answering these questions is easy. For those who were brought up in a Christian home and raised going to church, these types of questions aren't as difficult to consider. However, many of us did not grow up in the ideal, Christian home. Some of us grew up in broken homes. Others have been burned by a church. Some of us are numbing the pain and attempting to calm the nerve with alcohol, nicotine, sleeping around, or drugs. Everyone has to cope with life. Reality is not ideal for many people. The key to coping with the harsh realities of life is to do so in a way that is healthy and in a way that we know honors God.

One way I take a break from reality is by going to the movies. Recently, I have endeavored to start writing a movie script. This screenplay is a prophetic vision I have had for years that is starting to come to fulfillment. If I chose to live in the past, if I chose to go along with the rest of my family at times - and I love my family very much - then I would be snared to some serious generational curses. However, I've had to learn what I am telling you. It's time to let go of the past. It's time to grab hold of the future God has prepared for you.

When the devil comes at you with the past, with the sins of your own family members even, remind him of the Scriptures. Stand on God's Word. Don't embrace those generational curses that come down through the third and fourth generation. Instead, embrace your inheritance that is found in Jesus Christ. Take hold of the magnificent promises of God that last forever. To be clear: Generational curses do not mean God is against family! On the contrary, God desires to bless all families.

One reason the devil attacks the family unit is because the family unit is powerful. The family is where a person discovers their identity and is nurtured to full maturity. If the devil can dismantle the family, wreaking havoc anywhere he can, then he can hurt people. The devil's mode of operating is to hurt people. God uses the family to protect and preserve our lives. Whenever that family unit is broken, chaos and harm ensues. Divorce and family members turning on one another is heartbreaking to the Lord. If it grieves your soul, then it certainly grieves your Father's heart in Heaven.

The Bible is full of promises and commands regarding family. The promise for long life is found in Exodus 20:12 (NLT), which says, "Honor your father and mother. Then you will live a long, full life in the land the LORD your God is giving you." God commands us to honor our parents because He has made them custodians over our lives, especially when we are young. Parents serve a tremendous place in every person's life because it was ordained by God to be this way. When a parent or a child gets out of line, problems occur. These problems must be dealt with or the repercussions of bitterness, heartache, and even regret can last a lifetime.

Psalm 127:3-5 (NLT) tells us, "Children are a gift from the LORD; they are a reward from Him. Children born to a young man are like arrows in a warrior's hands. How joyful is the man whose quiver is full of them! He will not be put to shame when he confronts his accusers at the city gates." God has given man children to be a defense and a blessing in this world. God's will is to bless the family line. His desire is for His truth and His blessings to carry from one generation to the next. The generational curse is broken by passing the truth of God and His Word from one generation to the next.

The psalmist declares in Psalm 78:1-7 (NIV), "My people, hear my teaching; listen to the words of my mouth. I will open my mouth with a parable; I will utter hidden things, things from of old—things we have heard and known, things our ancestors have told us. We will not hide them from their descendants; we will tell the next generation the praiseworthy deeds of the Lord, His power, and the wonders He has done. He decreed statutes for Jacob and established the law in Israel, which He commanded our ancestors to teach their children, so the next generation would know them, even the children yet to be born, and they in turn would tell their children. Then they would put their trust in God and would not forget His deeds but would keep His commands."

Friend, you carry the praise of God in you. Your family duty is to pass His truth on from one generation to the next by honoring His Word. As the Scriptures say in Psalm 100:5 (NIV), "For the LORD is good and His love endures forever; His faithfulness continues through all generations." The praise you make today will carry forward to the generations that follow you. Your words carry creative power. When you give God the glory for what He has done in your life, you are setting a precedent for Him to do even greater things in the future.

The Apostle Paul tells us in 2 Corinthians 3:17-18 (ESV), "Now the Lord is the Spirit, and where the Spirit of the Lord is, there is freedom. And we all, with unveiled face, beholding the glory of the Lord, are being transformed into the same image from one degree of glory to another. For this comes from the Lord who is the Spirit." The Spirit of God is the One who sets us free from the generational curses that are plaguing our lives. The Spirit of the Lord reinstates a generational blessing that overrides the curse invoked by breaking the law of God.

Right now I believe God is breaking the yoke of poverty and releasing financial blessings that will carry down your generational line far past just the third or fourth generation. God is restoring your health and putting an end to generational illnesses that have been passed down genetically. The Lord is removing sexual immorality from your family line. He is breaking addictions, bad habits, and wrong thinking that has plagued your family tree for years. All of these yokes, or curses, are covered under the blood of Jesus.

Your sins have been paid for in full. Your sins have been forgiven. The generational curses stop with you. Your bloodline is loaded with blessings and favor. Your DNA is being recoded by God and programmed with blessings that the enemy cannot stop. Your decision today to follow Jesus Christ and to honor God and His Word is a decision that is unlocking not just blessings today but blessings for future generations to come.

Today receive your healing (Psalm 103:3). Receive the shalom peace of God into your heart and mind (Philippians 4:7). Entrust your soul to His ever-loving care (1 Peter 4:19). Allow Him to work out His promises in your life from the inside out. Your Creator is faithful. He will never leave you nor forsake you (Hebrews 13:5). He is going to do all that He has said He is going to do in your life and in the generations that are to follow.

SCRIPTURE READING

Exodus 20:4-6

Exodus 34:4-7

John 9:1-7

Galatians 3:7-14

QUESTIONS TO ANSWER

What are some generational curses that come to mind in your family line that need to be broken in Jesus' name?

What are practical steps you can take to remove yourself from toxic behavior in your family (or not participate in), so you can live in a way that honors God?

What are ways you can show love to your family members, even if they are not serving God, and still follow Christ without compromise?

Chapter Two
DECLARING GENERATIONAL BLESSINGS

When God does something, He first speaks it. God's words are words that carry authority and creative power. When God created the earth and all we see today, He first spoke it into existence. In the same way, God has given us a mouth to speak words of authority. As a child of God made in His image, your words are powerful. Declaring generational blessings is something you should train your mind to do every single day.

Every morning when I wake up, I say a prayer. In this prayer, I go down a list of blessings and promises God has made to us as heirs to His kingdom. I thank the Lord that I am the head and not the tail, that I am above and never beneath, that I shall lend and not borrow, that I shall ride on the heights of the earth, and that everything I touch shall prosper and succeed (from Deuteronomy 28). I thank the Lord for causing me to bear more good fruit and list the fruit of the Spirit out loud (Galatians 5:22-23). Then I thank the Lord for the nine spiritual gifts (1 Corinthians 12:8-10) and the seven gifts in Romans 12:6-8 and say all of them out loud.

There are many other Scriptures I pray aloud by memory every single day right after waking up. Now why in the world would I spend at least 15 to 20 minutes every morning going into great detail and great length rattling off all the different spiritual gifts, fruits, and blessings I have found throughout the Scriptures before going about my day? Why not just read it once at church, and that's that? The reason I speak these various gifts and blessings is because every day is a new day. If I don't speak the blessings, the devil and his army - along with the rest of the world - are going to speak the curses over me instead.

Friends, we are in a war. We aren't going to be living in a day of evil sometime in the future. We are living in the days of evil right now (Ephesians 5:16, 6:13). This means if we aren't on guard, if we aren't using our words and our faith to advance our lives and God's kingdom, then we are essentially moving backward. I have always been fascinated, and a little disturbed, by World War 2. During World War 2, Hitler and the Nazi army were on the offense, looking to drive out their enemies in every direction. It took years for the Nazis to be stopped, and it only happened because ally nations finally joined forces and fought back against this great evil.

In the same way, the devil is on the offense. He will take over as much territory as we let him. If you aren't using the Word of God, if you aren't declaring His truth over your life, then the devil is working overtime to take over your home turf. Satan doesn't want just bits and pieces of your life. He wants all of it. He wants to kill, steal, and destroy you because you are in God's Army (John 10:10). The good news today is the war has already been won! When Jesus Christ defeated death on the Cross, the war ended. Now we are learning to walk in this new identity of victory we have in Christ.

As we grow in our knowledge of the Word and who we are in Christ, we learn how to defeat the enemy and walk in our identity as a believer. Job 22:27-28 (NKJV) says, "You will make your prayer to Him, He will hear you, and you will pay your vows. You will also declare a thing, and it will be established for you; so light will shine on your ways." When you declare something from the Scriptures or something that God stirs up within you, there is an establishment that happens. You can establish a generational blessing based on what comes out of your mouth.

One of the most popular blessings declared over Jewish families and their descendants, and now many churches, is from Numbers 6:24-26 (NIV) which says, "The Lord bless you and keep you; the Lord make His face shine on you and be gracious to you; the Lord turn His face toward you and give you peace." When Moses tells Aaron and the priests to bless the Israelites this way, Moses also says why they are to declare these things. He says in Numbers 6:27 (NASB95), "So they shall invoke My name on the sons of Israel, and I then will bless them."

There is great power in God's name! In Christ, we now carry His name. Jesus also talks about the power of His name, the name that invokes and causes blessings on God's people. He says in John 17:12 (NKJV), "While I was with them in the world, I kept them in Your name. Those whom You gave Me I have kept; and none of them is lost except the son of perdition, that the Scripture might be fulfilled." There is supernatural protection when we speak the name of Jesus. When we call on God and read the Word, we are surrounded and guarded by His awesome presence and His holy name.

The name of Jesus is your identity. The name of Jesus is your authority when you pray and declare the blessing. The name of Jesus is how you defeat the enemy every single time. The Apostle Paul tells us in Philippians 2:8-9 (NASB95), "Being found in appearance as a man, He humbled Himself by becoming obedient to the point of death, even death on a cross. For this reason also, God highly exalted Him, and bestowed on Him the name which is above every name."

Because Jesus' name is above all names, His name is more powerful than any person, any demon, any legion, any government, and even any angels. His name holds the most authority in both the natural and spiritual realms. The biggest generational blessing you can give to your children, grandchildren, and those to come is the name of Jesus. Having a Christian legacy to hand to the next generation is the best gift you can give your family.

The blessings promised to Abraham and his descendants are now yours and your loved ones through Jesus. This means any blessing you read about in the Bible from either the Old or New Testament now belongs to you. You just have to take hold of the blessing, believe the blessing, speak the blessing, and let the blessing take root in your life.

Galatians 3:14 (NLT) says, "Through Christ Jesus, God has blessed the Gentiles with the same blessing He promised to Abraham, so that we who are believers might receive the promised Holy Spirit through faith." The blessings of Abraham now flow like water, which is the Holy Spirit deposited in our hearts (2 Corinthians 1:21-22), onto us and our family line. This means that we can speak what we desire to see. Whenever we have family members who are not saved or who are off course in life, we can pray and speak the opposite of what we see happening. We can stand in the gap and intercede for our loved ones.

Romans 4:17 (ESV) tells us, "As it is written, 'I have made you the father of many nations'—in the presence of the God in whom he believed, who gives life to the dead and calls into existence the things that do not exist." In Christ, we can speak into existence things that do not exist yet. This is why we speak healing whenever we are feeling sick or someone we are praying for is sick. This is why we speak prosperity and life over our finances and businesses. This is why we speak peace during times of conflict. We can alter the course of life by the words we declare in times of adversity.

When we speak what we do not physically see yet, we are operating in faith. Faith requires that we believe something before we actually see it. Faith is where the real power lies. Faith is what God requires in order for us to fulfill our destiny. As a matter of fact, anything that is not done from faith is actually sin (Romans 14:23). We are called to live a life based on faith and not mere physical sight (2 Corinthians 5:7).

Leaving a legacy of faith and love for God is the best legacy one can leave. Regardless of your age, when you choose to follow and serve the Living God, you are passing a generational blessing down to the next generation. Whether you have children or not, the people you impact and the blessings you impart go on through them. Your faith rubs off on others. God can do far more in and through you than you could ever imagine. The devil wants you to believe that you are ineffective and inadequate as a Christian. However, God says otherwise.

Ephesians 3:20-21 (NLT) encourages us, "Now all glory to God, who is able, through His mighty power at work within us, to accomplish infinitely more than we might ask or think. Glory to Him in the church and in Christ Jesus through all generations forever and ever! Amen." Throughout time, since the beginning of creation, all generations have one thing in common. Every generation had believers. Some generations had few, while others had many more. However, God has preserved faith in Him through every generation faithfully. Beginning with Adam and Eve, through all of the patriarchs, and later, Jesus' disciples - and now, us - faith in God has been passed on.

Throughout every generation God's power and glory has been demonstrated and seen in various ways. All generations can see the invisible attributes of God though the marvelous creation we see and experience every single day (Romans 1:20). Humankind has been given freewill. It is the one thing God will not violate. We all get the power of choice. Those who go to Heaven, it will be because they chose Jesus. For those who spend eternity in Hell, it will be because they chose to go there. They rejected Jesus.

God's will is that everyone would go to Heaven (see 2 Peter 3:9). However, God has given us the power of choice. He is not going to force you to love Him. The Lord will pursue us and stretch out His hand. He already displays His tremendous grace every day on the entire world. Psalm 145:9 (NLT) says, "The LORD is good to everyone. He showers compassion on all His creation."

The good news today is it's never too late to get back on the right course with God. Until a person's final breath, God's hand of mercy is extended to all. The eternal salvation Jesus offers is for everyone. No one is exempt or excluded from being eligible to receive God's grace. By putting your faith in Jesus, your sins are forgiven. You are made spotless and blameless in the eyes of God. All sins, failures, and mistakes are nailed to the Cross (Colossians 2:14). The debts you owe are paid for by Jesus. This is why when you come to Jesus, you are entitled to the generational blessings.

These blessings that have flowed from one generation to the next are now yours for the taking. When you receive and come into agreement with God's Word, there is great reward! King David declares in Psalm 19:8-11 (NLT), "The commandments of the Lord are right, bringing joy to the heart. The commands of the Lord are clear, giving insight for living. Reverence for the Lord is pure, lasting forever. The laws of the Lord are true; each one is fair. They are more desirable than gold, even the finest gold. They are sweeter than honey, even honey dripping from the comb. They are a warning to your servant, a great reward for those who obey them."

The way we see more of God's blessings and favor in our lives and in the lives of our families is by taking authority over what we speak. Our words have creative power. When you speak, speak life. I recently had a vision the Holy Spirit gave me. In this vision, I was carrying a megaphone. As I walked around with this megaphone, I saw various aspects of my life. I saw my work place. Then I saw my house. I saw my church. As I stood before these different places, I opened my mouth and declared, "LIFE."

As I spoke the word LIFE, the words traveled like sound waves creating a ripple effect. As the ripples traveled, they began to do their perfect work creating, you guessed it, life! The reason we live, breathe, and have our being is because God speaks life over us. He is our oversight. He is the Good Shepherd (John 10:11). He has told us what is good and what is bad. He is the Word, and His Word is our standard (John 1:1). When God speaks, He establishes rules and boundaries that, when broken, create a ripple effect of problems. On the contrary, these rules and boundaries, when respected and honored, create a ripple effect of blessings.

The ripple effect of our words and decisions by choosing to honor God is what causes generational blessings to flow. There is a posterity, which means all future generations of people, God has set aside for Himself and for His perfect work. You and I are part of this posterity through Christ. When we pray and speak by faith, we are creating faith and blessings that are going to move into the future. Here is the test: will you speak the blessing when everything seems the opposite?

In other words, will you declare healing and life when you are combating disease and death? It's easy to declare blessings when things are going well, when the sun is shining and the birds are chirping. However, when conflict builds and the clouds swell in darkness, this is when we really must dig in and speak words of faith and life. It is in these dark hours that the depths of our faith and character are tested and refined.

What you say in the war bunker during the heat of battle matters. What you pray when you see someone you love going the wrong way and making poor choices can alter the course of that person's life. Your words can turn the rudder of a great ship (James 3:4-5). Redemption for our family lines starts with us. It starts with the words that are coming out of our mouths. We must make the choice to stop speaking the curses and start speaking the blessings. We must move out of cynicism and criticism into a place of faith and victory.

The world will tell you that you are stuck with sin. You are "born this way". The truth is we are all born into sin (Psalm 51:5). You may have been born with a sharp tongue and a stubborn mindset, but in Christ you are something else altogether. You are a new creation (2 Corinthians 5:17). The only way the world is going to know Jesus is alive is through His people. If we are not breaking off generational curses, changing our demeanor even - stepping away from the harsh, critical attitude of this world - then we are no different from someone who is not following Jesus Christ.

Our words and what we speak should be very different from the words we hear while out in the world. You are living in today's culture, but you don't have to kneel to it. Be like Shadrach, Meshach, and Abednego. Refuse to bow. Stand firm in your faith. Don't let the world's standards bring you lower. Fill your mind and heart with God's standards, which is His Word, and rise above. Be an eagle and soar. Grab your megaphone and start declaring, "LIFE!!!"

You are walking in the generational blessings of Abraham, Isaac, and Jacob because of who you are in Christ. You are an heir to God's Kingdom. This means you are a king, you are a queen, in the eternal spiritual realm. Up in Heaven, you literally have a throne. There is a seat with your name on it that you are going to rule from as one of God's children for all eternity (Ephesians 2:6). Jesus is the first fruits, the firstborn, of this new spiritual creation we now walk in. Our identity is not determined by our carnal, fleshly nature. It's determined by the Spirit of Christ who dwells in our hearts.

The next time you are listening to a sermon or reading your Bible, remember who your ancestors are. Abraham is your grandfather in the faith. Sarah is your grandmother. All those who have gone before you are your aunts, uncles, and true family members in the faith (Matthew 12:48-50). Samson is your super strong relative who took out a thousand of his enemies with the jawbone of a donkey (Judges 15:16, Hebrews 11:32-33).

These men and women set a level of faith for you and those after you to walk in. Their stories aren't just stories. Their faith is your inheritance. You are next in their generational line. You are their posterity God promised to them. You are of tremendous value to God and so are those who are to follow you. Keep speaking the blessings. When you do, you are passing down life to the next generation.

SCRIPTURE READING

Deuteronomy 7:7-15

Numbers 6:22-27

Hebrews 11:39-40

Romans 4:16-18

QUESTIONS TO ANSWER

What are some generational blessings that come to mind in your family line?

What are some specific words of LIFE that you can begin to speak over your life and the lives of others?

What is a "ripple effect" blessing *(that is, a generational blessing)* you are walking in today because someone older than you chose to honor God?

Chapter Three
HOW TO PROPHESY

"Earnestly desire the spiritual gifts, especially that you may prophesy."
1 Corinthians 14:1

When the Apostle Paul gives this instruction to the Church, he highlights arguably the most powerful of all the spiritual gifts in our Holy Spirit arsenal. The reason the gift of prophecy is so powerful is because prophecy is a collection of words that release creative power. The direction of our lives is dictated by the words that are coming out of our mouths. When we speak, we are speaking either life or death, blessings or curses (Proverbs 18:21). This is why we need to examine the words that are coming out of our mouth.

One of the ministries (besides writing) that God has given me is the prophetic ministry. For years I have known that I was a prophet. For those who are unfamiliar with the fivefold ministry (apostles, prophets, evangelists, teachers, and pastors - see Ephesians 4:11), the office of the prophet is a position in the body of Christ that reports what he or she is seeing and hearing in the Spirit. Virtually my whole life I have been very sensitive to the spiritual realm. I would know things before they ever happened.

It wasn't until I began to discover the gift of prophecy and had other Spirit-filled believers continually tell me I was a prophet (which sounded so weird when they first spoke that over me!) that the anointing in the prophetic gifting began to flow naturally. God's desire is that every single person in the church would encounter, experience, and operate on some level in the gift of prophecy. If you have accepted Jesus Christ as your personal Lord and Savior, and you can speak words with your mouth, then you can prophesy.

The purpose of prophecy in the church is simple: It encourages us. 1 Corinthians 14:3 (NCV) tells us, "Those who prophesy are speaking to people to give them strength, encouragement, and comfort." One reason prophecy isn't as prevalent in many of the churches today is because the adversary has worked overtime to try and convince religious leaders that the spiritual gifts are dead. If the devil can take away the church's spiritual weapons of war, like the gift of prophecy, tongues, and all the others, then he can take away his enemy's guns.

We are the devil's enemy. He does not want us to prophesy. When we speak prophetic words, we dismantle darkness. We release breakthroughs and light in dark places. Through prophecy we can turn the tide of the battle. Droughts can be broken through prophets. Just ask Elijah. James 5:17-18 (NIV) tells us, "Elijah was a human being, even as we are. He prayed earnestly that it would not rain, and it did not rain on the land for three and a half years. Again he prayed, and the heavens gave rain, and the earth produced its crops."

The words you speak are powerful. Your words can shut up the heavens. Your words can shut up finances. Your words can cripple other people. However, your words can also do the opposite. When you speak words of life, the rain clouds can begin to form. Your access to resources becomes much broader. Those around you can begin to thrive by your words of affirmation and approval. We must train our minds to speak and decree the Word of God.

Anything we grew up hearing, saying, or believing that contradicts the promises of God must be corrected in our thinking. As I have grown in the prophetic gifting over the years, one thing I have learned is that when I actually start prophesying and encouraging others it is like turning on the water faucet. The Lord will start giving me more and more specific words, Scriptures, pictures, and even movie analogies to share with others. He will give these prophetic revelations concerning what is going on in my personal life as well.

There is nothing more empowering and life-giving than receiving a prophetic revelation from the Lord! It is God's will that all of us would operate in the prophetic gift. I think sometimes we make the gift of prophecy more complicated than it should be. One way you can learn to prophesy is simple. It's like anything else. Try it. Get around other believers, and ask God to give you a prophetic word or a prophetic picture for the person you are praying for. See what happens.

When I was in college, some buddies and I started a small group from the church. Several guys in the group weren't very familiar with the gifts of the Holy Spirit, like prophecy, praying in tongues, visions, and interpretations. However, as we all began to pray over each other each week, the Lord will begin to give different guys pictures and Scriptures and words for the person we were praying over. Before long, it was no big deal to receive a prophetic word from someone in the group. We had become more acquainted with the gift, and it certainly helped us grow leaps and bounds in our walks with Christ.

Acts 15:32 (NLT) says, "Then Judas and Silas, both being prophets, spoke at length to the believers, encouraging and strengthening their faith." Today God has filled the church with prophets, as well as pastors, teachers, evangelists, and even apostles, to encourage and strengthen the Body of Christ. The more the churches tap into this wonderful gift of prophecy, the more we are going to see revival and real life transformation in our communities. The older I get, the more I have learned that it is best to not hold back. Of course, I must exercise wisdom and be meek when I deliver a prophetic word. However, if I want God to develop this gifting in me, I must be using it and using it often.

When I was really young, I wanted to be the next Larry Bird. I would dribble, shoot free throws and layups, go to basketball camp, and practice in the back yard for hours on end. My parents would have to bribe me to come in when it was after dark because I loved playing basketball so much. I was addicted to the sport, and I was really good at it for being so young. In the same way, if you want to learn how to prophesy, you must practice. As you learn to operate in and use the gift, you will grow in it. Furthermore, you will be amazed whenever one of those prophetic words excites and encourages the one you are prophesying over.

A few years ago Pastor Clint asked me to have a Night of Prophecy at the church. I had never had a formal Night of Prophecy at the time, but it had been prophesied years ago at the Pasadena International House of Prayer (PIHOP) that one day I would minister before churches. The first Night of Prophecy was incredible. For two hours God showed me specific things about each person in the room. The participants were encouraged to turn on the recorder on their phones, so they could listen to their prophecies again in the future.

Since then we have held a Night of Prophecy about three times a year, and each time the Spirit of the Lord shows up and works mightily. We have seen marvelous prophetic fulfillments since we began these special times of ministry. While I am prophesying over people, many times I don't even know what I am saying. I just open my mouth, and God fills it with words. My carnal logic isn't even there. It is just God delivering His word through me. Sometimes God will give me strong impressions or cause me to be overwhelmed with a sensation to deliver the word He has for someone or for the church at large.

One time I started stomping my foot, and God said He was shaking the earth. I prophesied that He was causing earthquakes in places like Europe even right then. It was a totally spontaneous prophecy. The next day I got a screenshot of earthquakes from a friend who was attending the service, and she showed me where that very night before there were earthquakes in Europe and North Africa! As a prophet, I cannot always explain why God shows me certain things. I just deliver the message. Of course, it is always exciting whenever I have the privilege of getting to hear about prophetic words being fulfilled, but sometimes I never know. I just speak what the Spirit prompts me to speak.

While everyone is not called to be a prophet, or to hold the office of the prophet in the church, everyone has the prophetic gifting on them. The way we can all partake in the gift of prophecy is by getting around Spirit-filled believers who are prophesying. This is what happened to Saul and his messengers who weren't even on good terms with God at the time they were prophesying! 1 Samuel 19:20-24 (NASB95) tells us, "Then Saul sent messengers to take David, but when they saw the company of the prophets prophesying, with Samuel standing and presiding over them, the Spirit of God came upon the messengers of Saul; and they also prophesied.

When it was told Saul, he sent other messengers, and they also prophesied. So Saul sent messengers again the third time, and they also prophesied. Then he himself went to Ramah and came as far as the large well that is in Secu; and he asked and said, 'Where are Samuel and David?' And someone said, 'Behold, they are at Naioth in Ramah.' He proceeded there to Naioth in Ramah; and the Spirit of God came upon him also, so that he went along prophesying continually until he came to Naioth in Ramah. He also stripped off his clothes, and he too prophesied before Samuel and lay down naked all that day and all that night. Therefore they say, 'Is Saul also among the prophets?'"

One of the reasons this story is in the Bible is because it shows how powerful the anointing is. Whenever we get around a powerful anointing, that anointing takes over. This is what happens on the Night of Prophecy when I am ministering. The Spirit of the Lord is so strong that His authority just takes over. This is why praise and worship is so powerful. Whenever we allow ourselves to let go and worship God from the bottom of heart with no reservations, the Holy Spirit is free to move about and do powerful works that go beyond human logic and reason.

The truth is God's Spirit contradicts our carnal minds. Romans 8:7 (NIV) says, "The mind governed by the flesh is hostile to God; it does not submit to God's law, nor can it do so." One of the recurring visions I have with people who base everything purely on human logic is a wall I can see in their mind. The wall is their human logic blocking the things of the Spirit - but behind this "logic wall", there is this vast space of faith. When I prophesy, I have to speak past that human logic wall into the person's faith. When words of faith are spoken and released, it stirs up faith God has already instilled in us.

When prophecy hits the person directly in the heart, that's when the door of faith busts open in their soul. 1 Corinthians 14:24-25 (ESV) tells us, "But if all prophesy, and an unbeliever or outsider enters, he is convicted by all, he is called to account by all, the secrets of his heart are disclosed, and so, falling on his face, he will worship God and declare that God is really among you." Truly, when a prophet is speaking, the Holy Spirit is revealing the secret things inside the one who is being prophesied over.

One of the most dramatic and incredible prophecies I can recall recently is at a Night of Prophecy a couple of years ago. I was going around the room speaking what God was showing me in the Spirit over those in attendance, as well as over anyone else who wanted a word but wasn't in attendance. While ministering I began to literally feel pregnant! I immediately knew this word was for my dear friend Lee, who also operates strongly in the prophetic ministry.

I began to laugh because I knew this word was going to blow Lee away. When I finished laughing uncontrollably (which tends to happen when the joy of the Lord is filling up the room!) and regained my composure, I finally asked Lee if she had a daughter. Her eyes got really big, and she said yes. Then I proceeded to tell her that she was going to be a grandma soon. Lee nearly fell out of the pew! I then said, as to console her, that I didn't know when but sometime in the future. That prophetic word was delivered in October.

By December, Lee's daughter shocked mom and dad by telling them she was pregnant. Needless to say, the prophet (yours truly) got a phone call from Lee shortly after the bombshell announcement at Christmas supper. About nine months after the prophetic word was delivered to grandma "Lou Lou" Lee one of the most beautiful babies in the world was born! The prophetic word given in October was fulfilled. Today Lee is the happiest Lou Lou in the world. I have no doubt God has an incredible plan for this miracle of a child whose arrival was pre-announced through a word of prophecy.

No one ever said delivering a prophetic word cannot be fun, special, or amazing. Operating in the gifts of the Holy Spirit is awesome and meant to be experienced with great joy. This is why the Scriptures say, "Be full of joy in the Lord always. I will say again, be full of joy." (Philippians 4:4 NCV) Being in the presence of the Lord and experiencing prophetic ministry with other believers is meant to be full of joy overflowing. Heaven is full of joy, singing, and celebration. Our sanctuaries here on earth should be no different!

The key to learning about and operating in the gift of prophecy begins and continues by spending time with God every single day. When you make it top priority to read the Bible and pray every day, the Spirit of God in you is being stirred up. The Holy Spirit will begin to reveal things to you. When you seek the Lord, that is when you will get the prophetic revelation. It takes time, energy, and sacrifice to get to a place spiritually where you can experience the flow of this encouraging gift.

Make it your goal to eliminate distractions and the noise of the world to be with God. One of the best ways I can hear God is when I am resting on my bed with no distractions. The Lord can speak to you anywhere at any time. However, learning how God speaks to you is a personal experience between you and the Lord. God speaks in so many different ways. He shows some people pictures in their minds. Some He will give a specific word or phrase. Others He will give a Scripture that applies to the situation at hand.

Hebrews 1:1-2 (NIV) tells us, "In the past God spoke to our ancestors through the prophets at many times and in various ways, but in these last days He has spoken to us by His Son, whom He appointed heir of all things, and through whom also He made the universe." Through Christ all believers have the ability to receive prophetic revelation in various ways. The Holy Spirit came from Heaven on Pentecost in order to dwell in the hearts of all who believe. The Holy Spirit already knows all things. However, we must tap into this river of living water.

Jesus stood and declared during the great Feast of Booths, "If anyone is thirsty, let him come to Me and drink. He who believes in Me, as the Scripture said, 'From his innermost being will flow rivers of living water.'" (John 7:37-38 NASB95) The river of living water is what gives our souls life. This river is what gives us prophetic dreams and visions. The outpouring of God's Spirit is happening as you read this. We are living in the last hour, when all of God's children will prophesy and have dreams (Acts 2:17-18). It's time to jump in the river and let His Spirit flow in and through our lives.

Today receive the prophetic gift in Jesus' name. Invite the Holy Spirit, the living water of God, to give you prophetic revelation. Listen for His voice (John 10:27). Be attentive to what He is showing you on the movie screen of your mind. Pay attention to the atmosphere around you as the Holy Spirit reveals His divine presence. Go to sleep ready to receive prophetic dreams. Wake up anticipating to hear God's voice (Psalm 5:3). You are the vessel God has chosen to speak and make His words known.

SCRIPTURE READING

1 Samuel 19:19-24

Numbers 11:24-29

1 Corinthians 14:1-5

Acts 2:17-18

QUESTIONS TO ANSWER

Do you earnestly desire to have more of the spiritual gifts?

What are some ways you can grow in the gift of prophecy? *(For example: by praying more with others who are seeking God with you.)*

Have you ever had a dream you felt like was from God? What do you think God was trying to show you from the dream?

Chapter Four
LEADERSHIP

We live in a culture that lauds financial success, independence, and winning. The pride of life rules much of the world today (1 John 2:16). While success in and of itself is not evil, priorities out of order can definitely carry anyone down the wrong path. Jesus tells us that our biggest priority is to live for God. Furthermore, the goal in life is not to have everyone serve us and praise us, but rather we are to serve others and praise God.

Jesus says in Matthew 23:11-12 (NIV), "The greatest among you will be your servant. For those who exalt themselves will be humbled, and those who humble themselves will be exalted." According to God and His Word, true leadership is characterized by humility and service. If anyone desires to be in a position of leadership, they must first develop a servant's heart. Without a heart that desires to serve others, a person is not fit to be a good leader.

Bad leaders are self-seeking and power hungry. Examples of poor leadership abound. Politicians are arguably the most untrustworthy people on the planet. Many leaders in government are grossly overpaid, only promote agendas that will get themselves re-elected, and talk out of both sides of their mouth. A lack of the fear of the Lord and a lack of true humility is the problem with our leaders today. Jesus turned the world upside down when He taught on what leadership is.

The disciples had an argument over leadership when they began to discuss who was greatest in God's Kingdom. Luke 22:24-26 (NLT) tells us, "Then they began to argue among themselves about who would be the greatest among them. Jesus told them, 'In this world the kings and great men lord it over their people, yet they are called 'friends of the people.' But among you it will be different. Those who are the greatest among you should take the lowest rank, and the leader should be like a servant.'" Jesus Christ is our Leader. When Jesus came to the earth, He came to serve. He is the example of perfect leadership.

In the same way, if we want to stand out from the crowd, if we desire to lead, we must first serve. Leaders lead in order to serve. When leadership misses this principle, they are no longer fit to be a good leader. We see people who obtain great success all the time in the media - then we see these same people whom the world says "got it all" fall. They end up on drugs. Their lives fall apart. They're being arrested and carried off from a night club. What happened? The success got to their head. As the proverb goes, "Pride goes before destruction, and a haughty spirit before a fall." (Proverbs 16:18 ESV)

The higher you rise in life, the lower you must go in spirit. This is what it means in the beatitudes when Jesus says, "Blessed are the poor in spirit, for theirs is the kingdom of Heaven." (Matthew 5:3 ESV) When we get on our face in prayer, humble before the Lord, this is the most powerful place we can be. We have our Creator's attention when we have things in proper perspective. True leaders pray, and pray a lot. God desires for His children to rise to positions of authority and leadership in this world. However, He is not going to cause us to go up higher if we have bad attitudes and a prideful heart.

God wants us to lead by serving. Furthermore, He wants us to have a diligent spirit. The Apostle Paul tells us that the one who has the spiritual gift of leadership is to lead with diligence (Romans 12:8). When God established the family unit - the husband, the wife, and their children - He named the man as head of household. The leader of the house is meant to be the father. The reason the man is to be the head of the house is because the man is expected to be selfless - the one who leads by serving and by doing what is in the very best interest of his wife and children.

Many men have dropped the ball in being head of household today because men have stopped going to church. They have stopped being the spiritual leader in the home and have therefore lost their God-given role as the household leader. Because we have a culture that no longer observes the Word and has distorted Biblical truth, many homes are broken and out of order. I have lived this reality myself - having come from a home where my parents have been divorced (and more than once!).

The good news today is the broken home can stop with you. If you are a man, you can step up and become the man God created you to be. You can be the diligent hand and the leader of the home. If you are a woman, you can step up and empower your husband to become the leader of your home by praying for and supporting him. It starts by seeking to honor the Lord, one step at a time. If you are living together with your partner out of wedlock, then it's time to either decide to get married or cut ties with each other if you aren't going to make it right before God. The Lord desires to bless your home, but you must do your part and get into alignment with His Word.

The culture has taught us that marriage is breakable and even unnecessary for two people who are "in love". Couples live together for years, sometimes raise children together, and never tie the knot. This is not pleasing to God. The Bible tells us in Hebrews 13:4 (NIV), "Marriage should be honored by all, and the marriage bed kept pure, for God will judge the adulterer and all the sexually immoral." Sin always carries a price. No one escapes God's judgment. The reason the Lord has allowed much to go on like He has is because He is being merciful (Romans 11:32). However, there comes a day when God's mercy is up, and His justice shows up.

The best thing you can do for you and your family is make things right before God. When there is proper leadership in the home, it enables everyone to prosper and thrive. Ephesians 5:24-25 (NIV) says, "Now as the church submits to Christ, so also wives should submit to their husbands in everything. Husbands, love your wives, just as Christ loved the church and gave Himself up for her." Marriages work when Christ is the center of them. Remove Christ from the center of the marriage, and the carnal man and the carnal woman come out to argue and fight. The man's duty is to love his wife as himself, and the wife's duty is to respect her husband (Ephesians 5:33).

Being a leader means being an overseer. A leader is always looking for ways to protect others from harm and to guide people to safe pastures. The Apostle Paul tells the Church in Acts 20:28 (NASB95), "Be on guard for yourselves and for all the flock, among which the Holy Spirit has made you overseers, to shepherd the church of God which He purchased with His own blood." Being spiritually safe is extremely important. There are so many false doctrines and false religions in the world that anyone can be led astray who is not firmly rooted and grounded in faith. God has planted leadership within the church in order to help others in their walk with God.

The enemy is always looking for ways to take down God's people. The Apostle Paul goes on to say in Acts 20:29-31 (NASB95), "I know that after my departure savage wolves will come in among you, not sparing the flock; and from among your own selves men will arise, speaking perverse things, to draw away the disciples after them. Therefore be on the alert, remembering that night and day for a period of three years I did not cease to admonish each one with tears." Leaders aren't afraid to put up a fight to protect their own. Leaders protect and defend the ones entrusted to their care. The Apostle Paul continually protected God's people. He taught, encouraged, and warned the churches continually during his time of ministry. Those in leadership must be on the alert and ready.

Furthermore, leadership should keep sober. Proverbs 31:4-5 (NLT) tells us, "It is not for kings, O Lemuel, to guzzle wine. Rulers should not crave alcohol. For if they drink, they may forget the law and not give justice to the oppressed." Leaders are called to live by a higher standard than others. Leaders are willing to give up their own rights for the sake of others. How you lead today will impact the generations that follow. If you make it a habit to drink and live a reckless life, you are passing this lifestyle on to the next generation. If you make it a habit to instill values in your children and do your best to honor God, you are passing on a legacy that will endure for many generations to come (Deuteronomy 7:9).

Leaders are spokespersons. Moses is an excellent example of a spokesperson from the Scriptures. Moses interceded and spoke on behalf of the people to God continually. It is through Moses that God gave us the Ten Commandments (Exodus 20:1-17). Through Moses, God delivered His people out of slavery in Egypt. Leaders are called to speak on behalf of the people. Whenever a person is called to a position of leadership, they usually must go through a process of refinement before they step into a position of power.

All of the good leaders we see throughout the Scriptures were greatly humbled or already humble in heart when they were called to lead. The Bible says in Numbers 12:3 (NIV), "Now Moses was a very humble man, more humble than anyone else on the face of the earth." God chose Moses because of his humility. Likewise, God chose Gideon because Gideon did not rely on his own strength or confidence. As a matter of fact, Gideon was fearful to the point of behaving cowardly towards his enemies and even his own family (Judges 6:27). Gideon knew he needed God. One of the attributes of genuine humility in a person is when they know how much they truly need the Lord.

Those who rely on their own strength and power are not the ones God is looking for to lead. God is looking for an obedient heart and a willing spirit. He is looking for those who do what He says to do. 2 Chronicles 16:9 (NLT) tells us, "The eyes of the LORD search the whole earth in order to strengthen those whose hearts are fully committed to Him." When we lay aside our worries, concerns, and daily chores in order to put God first in our lives, our lives are going to start to fall into order God's way. This is why Jesus says in Matthew 6:33 (NKJV), "But seek first the kingdom of God and His righteousness, and all these things shall be added to you."

Leaders bring out the best in people. Leaders are always looking out for others. The Apostle Paul says in Philippians 2:3-4 (NASB95), "Do nothing from selfishness or empty conceit, but with humility of mind regard one another as more important than yourselves; do not merely look out for your own personal interests, but also for the interests of others." Natural born leaders have an ability to call out greatness in others. This is why mentors, coaches, and school teachers are so powerful. When a student or an athlete first comes under their instruction, they aren't as skilled. They may have no knowledge on the subject matter or not be physically fit enough for the sport.

However, as these leaders begin to train their students, they become more knowledgeable. They become more physically fit and trained to compete in the games. Good coaches, mentors, and teachers are able to help guide their students to greatness. The same is true for those in government. The best leaders not only create policies that make life better for the community, they also inspire their citizens to rise above and accomplish great things.

On the contrary, poor leadership is the opposite. Bad leaders oppress those whom they are called to lead. In the economy right now, we have high inflation, lower quality of life, and an administration that has disavowed the Word of God by all of the policies they have put into place. The result is a country that is suppressed by poor leadership. Proverbs 29:2 (NLT) defines well the current condition of our nation (as I am writing this): "When the godly are in authority, the people rejoice. But when the wicked are in power, they groan."

Lack of leadership causes people to become stagnant and unproductive. We see businesses fail all of the time from lack of leadership and solid vision. We even see churches fail or become stagnant from a lack of strong leadership. Every organization and every home needs good leadership to help guide people. Jesus is the ultimate leader everyone needs in their life. Matthew 9:36-38 (NIV) tells us, "When He [Jesus] saw the crowds, He had compassion on them, because they were harassed and helpless, like sheep without a shepherd [leader]. Then He said to His disciples, 'The harvest is plentiful but the workers are few. Ask the Lord of the harvest, therefore, to send out workers into His harvest field.'"

As we look at the condition of the world today, it is plain to see that there is a real lack of spiritual leadership and godly guidance in the culture. People are like lost sheep. People are so confused they don't even know their gender. A boy thinks he is a girl. A girl thinks she is a boy. Some people are so confused they don't even think they are human but a cat! We are taught the earth is billions of years old, and we somehow evolved from monkeys. Even within the church, we are told that the power and gifts of the Holy Spirit are dead since after the "apostolic era", and water baptism is salvation and not faith in Jesus Christ. All of these end times false beliefs are to be blamed in part on the Church and a lack of godly leadership.

The good news today is God has placed His seal on you (Ephesians 1:13). You are a natural born leader in Christ. When you were spiritually born again (1 Peter 1:23), you were born into a family of royal priests and spiritual leaders following the Spirit of Christ (Romans 8:14). You are the answer to the confusion in this world. You are God's answer to retrieving His lost sheep. When you do your best to honor God, you are being a part of the solution. You are acting as a good shepherd would.

You are Christ's ambassador (2 Corinthians 5:20). You are a spokesperson for Jesus Christ. It is God's will and good pleasure to make you one of His diplomats in the world, sent to call people home and bring them back to God their Father. You are one of the present day Deborahs, Josephs, and Daniels of the world. You are called to rise in your sphere of influence. When you carry an excellent spirit like your ancestors in the faith, God is causing all things to work together for your good (Romans 8:28).

The influence you carry is much greater than you realize. Your decisions and your voice will carry to future generations. The enemy may have done his best to silence you, to keep you from rising in influence and in leadership, but the anointing on you is unstoppable. You have the Holy Spirit working in you, causing you to change, transform, and rise higher. This is why the Apostle Paul says in Ephesians 3:20-21 (NLT), "Now all glory to God, who is able, through His mighty power at work within us, to accomplish infinitely more than we might ask or think. Glory to Him in the church and in Christ Jesus through all generations forever and ever! Amen."

Speak the Word of God over your life. Speak His Word over your parents, spouse, and children. Declare His Scriptures over your church, school, and community. God's Word is eternal. The angels of the Lord guard God's Word in order to perform what He says (Psalm 103:20). When you speak the promises of God, you are releasing power. You are charging the hosts of Heaven to go to work on your behalf. You are reminding God what He said He is going to do. You are strengthening your soul for the day of battle ahead.

You are a leader. You have an authorized position chosen by God to fill. Whether your role and calling is to be a mom, a grandparent, a teacher, a business leader, or a vocational minister, there is somewhere God has preordained for you to serve. Your service is to make the world a better place. You are the salt of the earth and the light of the world (Matthew 5:13-14). Your salt puts out fires and saves lives. Your light makes others' lives brighter.

When you serve others, you are being the best kind of leader there is. Looking to the needs of others to help them on their life journey is what God has called you to do. You are loaded with talent and creativity to fulfill the call of God on your life. You are rising higher and going to new levels of success as you keep your focus on Jesus and God's Holy Word.

SCRIPTURE READING

Numbers 12:1-8

2 Chronicles 16:7-9

Matthew 23:11-12

2 Corinthians 5:18-20

QUESTIONS TO ANSWER

What are some leadership traits you see in people around you that you can call out and encourage them in?

Who is a leader that you look up to? How can you pray for them as they lead others?

Where is a place that lacks good leadership that you can pray for and ask God to bring good leaders into? *(For example: a family home, a church, a business, government, etc.)*

Chapter Five
SERVANTHOOD

Jesus is the perfect model of servanthood. The Son of God chose to leave His heavenly abode, where He is wealthier than our wildest imaginations and more highly exalted than even the greatest of angels, and came to earth as a humble servant. Jesus did not come into the world as some rich king or glorious soldier. He came in meekness and gentleness. He did not come down here so that people would serve Him hand and foot, although He certainly deserves it!

Jesus says in Luke 22:27 (NIV), "For who is greater, the one who is at the table or the one who serves? Is it not the one who is at the table? But I am among you as one who serves." The entitlement attitude we see in the world is the opposite of Christ's attitude we read about in the Scriptures. Furthermore, anyone who is truly walking in the Spirit is going to have the same attitude as Jesus Christ. We are all called to servanthood.

The next time you are out dining, remember the words of Christ. In God's eyes, the one serving is just as important as the one who is seated at the table. God is not a respecter of people and neither should we be. On the contrary, God actually stands in opposition to the pompous and prideful (James 4:6). The Lord has a way of humbling anyone who needs it. There is no one on the planet God cannot make low. No matter how wealthy, politically powerful, entertaining, beautiful, smart, athletic, or influential a person is, God knows how to humble a prideful heart.

We are not in this world to only get. We are not here so we can be kings and queens that everyone caters to and bows down before. We are here to serve. We are here to display the love of God so that people may come to know Jesus Christ as their personal Lord and Savior. Whenever we miss this powerful truth, we have missed our calling. That's why a wonderful education and a great job or career does not matter if it is not used to glorify God. Olympic gold medals and million-dollar ideas are worthless if it's not used to glorify the Lord. Some of the wealthiest and most famous people in the world today are still empty on the inside. The reason is because they missed their calling.

Every single person was designed by the Creator in order to glorify Him in their own way. When a person only lives for self, the result is emptiness. No amount of worldly success is going to fill this void. We are here to make the world a better place by serving others. The Apostle Peter tells us in 1 Peter 4:10-11 (NIV), "Each of you should use whatever gift you have received to serve others, as faithful stewards of God's grace in its various forms. If anyone speaks, they should do so as one who speaks the very words of God. If anyone serves, they should do so with the strength God provides, so that in all things God may be praised through Jesus Christ. To Him be the glory and the power for ever and ever. Amen."

When a person uses their gifts and talents for personal gain and worldly agendas - and refuses to give the one true God all the glory - He gives them over to a reprobate mind (Romans 1:28). Instead of being used by the Lord, the enemy uses them. This is why the world is in turmoil today. Gender confusion, bloated government deficits, injustices in the court systems, redefining marriage, lauding immorality, money laundering, taking sides with Israel's enemies, all of these things are a result of people rejecting the Word of God. The level of deception continues to increase in these last days, as the Scriptures told us it would (2 Timothy 3:1,13).

The good news today is we can be the salt that gives the life and flavor of Christ in this world. We can dismantle and destroy the works of the enemy by learning and practicing ways to serve one another. God has set us in this world to shine bright in word and deed, even when it seems like we are surrounded by total darkness. Philippians 2:13-15 (NASB95) says, "For it is God who is at work in you, both to will and to work for His good pleasure. Do all things without grumbling or disputing; so that you will prove yourselves to be blameless and innocent, children of God above reproach in the midst of a crooked and perverse generation, among whom you appear as lights in the world."

When you keep your eyes set on Christ and on carrying about your heavenly Father's business, you are going to shine. It is impossible for you to behold the glory of God without His glory shining back down on you - just as the sun shines on the moon, and the moon reflects the sun's light. The more you set your mind and heart on serving Him, His light is going to start shining down on you. Others are going to see it. You are going to stand out from the rest of the world. Before King David ever became a great king - that is, a king with many warriors, chariots, horses, servants, and top national advisors at his full disposal - he had to serve.

When David had to serve, it was less than ideal. David served his father's household by protecting the sheep from the threat of lions and bears (1 Samuel 17:34-35). When David was promoted, he played music for a bipolar king named Saul (1 Samuel 16:23). After David found success on the battlefield, Saul became jealous and tried to pin him to the wall with his spear (1 Samuel 18:5-11). The one who initially promoted David into royal service became the one who spent years trying to kill him. David spent much of his life fleeing from his own countrymen and even his son Absalom. Because David had a heart that was full of worship and sought to serve the Lord, God delivered him every time.

The truth is we are all the servants of either one of two masters. The Apostle Paul explains the nature of sin saying in Romans 6:16-19 (NCV), "Surely you know that when you give yourselves like slaves to obey someone, then you are really slaves of that person. The person you obey is your master. You can follow sin, which brings spiritual death, or you can obey God, which makes you right with Him. In the past you were slaves to sin - sin controlled you. But thank God, you fully obeyed the things that you were taught. You were made free from sin, and now you are slaves to goodness. I use this example because this is hard for you to understand. In the past you offered the parts of your body to be slaves to sin and evil; you lived only for evil. In the same way now you must give yourselves to be slaves of goodness. Then you will live only for God."

If you are not following and serving the Lord, then you are following and serving your carnal nature. True Godly servanthood means we are listening to and obeying the Holy Spirit sent from Heaven to lead, guide, and direct us. Because we are living in the last days, the level of deception and forms of godliness (which is not true godliness) is only going to increase. 2 Timothy 3:5 says people will take on a form of religion or godliness but deny the power of God. There are many worldly agendas that appear good on the surface but are really from the enemy.

The climate change agenda and worship of "mother" earth, the "love is love" campaign that attempts to justify immorality, pro-choice being a right and a freedom that attempts to justify murdering the innocent, the propaganda constantly spewed out against Israel (the only democracy in the Middle East), wrongfully defunding entire police departments under the guise of racism, and other narratives we constantly hear about in the news, on social media, and on the airwaves are modern-day examples of a deceptive form of godliness but denying the truth.

The question we must ask ourselves is who are we serving? Are we serving the liberal (aka lawless), godless agendas in the air that seem good to our carnal nature, or are we serving the Living God who never deviates from His Word? The line has been drawn in the sand in this last hour. The enemy knows his time is short (Revelation 12:12). The level of deception between right and wrong is only going to increase in the coming days. The good news is we can arm ourselves in the Spirit for the upcoming spiritual battles. The victory is already won through what Jesus did on the cross.

Our faith is what defeats the enemy. When we set our sights above and seek to serve the Lord, He will show us what is happening in the Spirit. Having spiritual insight is invaluable to helping us navigate life's challenges. Time and again I have experienced personally and heard stories from others about God sending dreams. Throughout the Scriptures God sends His servants dreams in order to protect them, to warn them, to give them insight into what He is doing, and to encourage them. When I began writing this book "Generations", God confirmed I was to continue on writing by speaking through various people.

Over and over I would hear preachers and prophets talk about "generational lines". I found myself continually talking about the importance and the power of establishing a Godly generational family line. The Holy Spirit was bubbling up this important truth about His kingdom, that He places a strong value on generational lines. The Lord is all for protecting, preserving, and carrying forward families and their lineages. The Apostle Paul says in Ephesians 3:14-15 (NASB95), "For this reason I bow my knees before the Father, from whom every family in heaven and on earth derives its name."

When a family decides to be servants of God, the Lord anoints the family to be set apart for Kingdom purposes. Serving the Lord passes an inheritance and a heritage to the next generation of family members. This is why it is so important if you are a parent or grandparent to pray for your children and grandchildren. If you don't pray for your generational line, the enemy will do all he can to destroy it. Psalm 127:3-5 (NLT) tells us, "Children are a gift from the Lord; they are a reward from Him. Children born to a young man are like arrows in a warrior's hands. How joyful is the man whose quiver is full of them! He will not be put to shame when he confronts his accusers at the city gates."

Serving the Lord is a family thing. I have a good friend and his wife who recently began attending my home church. He operates strongly in the prophetic gifting like myself. He can literally go for hours sharing what the Spirit is saying. As I listen to him, he reveals things by the Spirit operating through him that are so specific, exact, and dead on. He is committed to serving the Lord and to being true to the word of God. As I have grown to learn more and more about him and his family, I have begun to see what a strong prophetic anointing there is on the entire family. I have even given prophetic words to him, his wife, and his children.

One thing I saw while ministering to him was this heavy anointing of the prophetic on the entire family unit! However, my brother in the Lord has shared several stories of him and different family members receiving false and distorted prophetic words in the past. These words have been damaging to different members of the family. They are still in the process of healing from some of them. I explained to my prophetic brother that the enemy has been on a tear trying to wipe out and destroy the prophetic anointing on the entire family. That is why the devil has worked overtime, even through others in ministry, trying to distort this powerful gifting on this amazing family.

Whenever a person has a strong anointing on their life from the Lord, the enemy will try to attack it. The longer I am in ministry, I have noted that the devil will always do the exact opposite of what God is doing in the person He has called. If a person has a calling to prosper, the devil will try to bring destruction and financial ruin. If a person has an anointing to pastor and lead a church, the enemy will try to tempt this leader away from their calling through sin. Everyone is in a battle for their anointing.

For years I was told that I have a "Joseph company" anointing. People would tell me they saw gold on my hands in the Spirit. Multiple people prophesied that I have a calling to Wall Street and to markets. At the time I received these words I was a beyond-poor college student. I was financially upside down. People spoke this so much over me that I actually began to resent the prophetic word, which the Lord tells us not to do by the way! 1 Thessalonians 5:20 tells us to not despise prophetic utterances. One reason these words (which were actually meant to encourage) frustrated me for quite some time is because my life looked totally opposite of what had been spoken.

Whenever God calls you to something, every time it will not have existed yet. If it already existed, you wouldn't need faith. You can already physically see it. No faith required. What I was going through was the test of faith. However, many years later I am now walking in the call of God on my life to investments and financial markets. I can now see the manifestation of what was seemingly impossible for me to see years before. I am now living the "Joseph company" life that was spoken into my life long ago. In the same way, there are prophetic words and anointings God is calling you to grow into.

The way I grew into this financial anointing is through serving in the marketplace. The best companies are built on excellent service. In economics, great service typically results in profitable business. God honors serving, even in the world of commerce. There is a reward for serving and meeting the needs of others. God is in the business of meeting needs (Philippians 4:19). Whatever God call you to do, it will always involve helping and serving others in some way. Your gifts and talents etched into your DNA are from the Lord.

When you read the Bible and get around other Spirit-filled believers who speak life into your soul, your gifts and talents are going to be drawn out. Many things in you are still a mystery. They must be brought forth by the Holy Spirit. This is why revelation is so powerful and so awesome. One of my favorite Scriptures about these kinds of revelations is found in the book of Jeremiah. The prophet declares in Jeremiah 33:3 (NASB), "Call to Me and I will answer you, and I will tell you great and mighty things, which you do not know."

Friend, there are so many things which you do not know that God wants to reveal to you. God's plans for you are marvelous! Serving the Lord is a lifelong journey of discovery and revelation. Jesus tells us in Matthew 6:33 (NKJV), "But seek first the kingdom of God and His righteousness, and all these things shall be added to you." God's kingdom is endless (see Isaiah 9:7). His dominion and rule is far greater than anything you could ever imagine. You have a right and an inheritance to this great Kingdom because you are in Christ.

As a servant of God, your job here on earth is never finished. There is always a next chapter. As long as you have air in your lungs, God has a reason for keeping you in this world. When you believe, all things are possible. Believing is what unlocks doors and releases the supernatural. Your story, which is really your testimony, matters. It matters to God, and it matters to others. When you share your story with others, it causes faith to rise. When faith rises, the power of God's kingdom can be released to do the impossible.

By serving the Living God, you are living out the belief that God is alive and at work. There is no better way to live than by trusting in the One who created it all. You are a walking testimony that God is alive. You are loaded with potential. You are made in His image. You are called to walk as Jesus walked, full of grace and full of truth (John 1:14). You have the mantle of faith entrusted to you that is being passed down from one generation of believers to the next.

I believe just as the Spirit of God hovered over the waters at the beginning of time, He is hovering over you (Genesis 1:2). He is doing a new thing in your life (Isaiah 43:19). New beginnings and new chapters are straight ahead. Your acts of service and kindness are noticed by God. You have not been ignored or left behind. The Lord has gone before you. He is making your crooked places straight. He is taking you from glory to glory.

SCRIPTURE READING

1 Samuel 17:31-37

Psalm 127:3-5

Luke 22:24-27

Romans 6:16-19

QUESTIONS TO ANSWER

Who are the people in your life today that God has called you to serve? *(For example: children, spouse, customers, church or community members, etc.)*

What is a word or promise you feel like is from the Lord that has not come to pass yet? Like David shepherding sheep before becoming a king, how can you stay faithful until that word or promise is fulfilled?

What is an anointing, or enabling, God has placed on your life that you could see the enemy trying to steal or attack *(like in the case of my friend and his family)*? How can you refine this gifting of the Lord to serve others?

Part Two

BELIEVE

"Do not be afraid; only believe."
Mark 5:36

Chapter Six
PASSING THE MANTLE

In life, there are always cycles and a change of leadership. The pendulum is always swinging. Opinions are always changing. Who is large and in charge today may not be tomorrow. Because nothing in life is permanent or guaranteed it is always a good idea to consider preparing for the future. This is what happened to the prophet Elijah when he had had enough of Jezebel and Ahab. Elijah had dealt with some of the most wicked leaders in human history, and he was ready to literally get off this huge rock called planet Earth. Ever been there? I know I have.

God honored Elijah's desire to "get outta here" and took Elijah up in His very own flaming chariot from Heaven (2 Kings 2:11). However, before Elijah left he made a wise decision. He chose someone to pass the mantle of Godly leadership onto for when he was no longer around. 1 Kings 19:19 (NKJV) says, "So he [Elijah] departed from there, and found Elisha the son of Shaphat, who was plowing with twelve yoke of oxen before him, and he was with the twelfth. Then Elijah passed by him and threw his mantle on him." What is profound about the timing of Elijah finding his successor as Israel's number one prophet is the twelfth yoke of oxen Elisha was with.

In Hebrew, the number twelve symbolizes the perfect government of God. Just as there are twelve tribes of Israel, twelve apostles, and twelve months in the year, there is a perfect order and government God has established in this world. The twelfth oxen symbolized God's establishment as Elijah was passing the mantle of prophet onto Elisha. During Elisha's stent as Elijah's servant and helper, he witnessed Elijah's power and anointing God had bestowed upon him.

Elisha knew Elijah had the power to call down fire from heaven and destroy Ahab's messengers twice (2 Kings 1:9-12). He knew Elijah convened and spoke with angels as he ministered (2 Kings 1:15). Just as Elisha's twelve sets of oxen were yoked together to get work done, so Elisha was yoked to Elijah for a set time to learn and help Elijah fulfill his mission. In the same way, we should all be looking at someone we can yoke ourselves to in order to grow in our faith. We should also look for someone we can reach out to that we can mentor and help raise up.

This multi-generational yoking together is how strong churches and strong believers are built. When a father teaches and raises up a son, the two grow together. The son learns from the father, and the father learns wisdom in dealing with the son. The perfect example of the father-son relationship is found in Jesus Christ, the Son of God, and God the Father. Jesus refers to and quotes the Father throughout His entire ministry. Jesus calls God His "Father" about 165 times in the Scriptures.

Jesus continually made it clear to His opponents that His authority came from His Father. John 8:26-30 (NLT) says, "'I have much to say about you and much to condemn, but I won't. For I say only what I have heard from the One who sent Me, and He is completely truthful.' But they still didn't understand that He was talking about His Father. So Jesus said, 'When you have lifted up the Son of Man on the cross, then you will understand that I am He. I do nothing on My own but say only what the Father taught Me. And the One who sent Me is with Me—He has not deserted Me. For I always do what pleases Him.' Then many who heard Him say these things believed in Him."

Jesus' mantle of authority was placed upon Him from God in Heaven. He is the example and perfect role model all believers should follow. When we begin to walk in the Spirit of Christ, we learn from the anointing that was planted deep within us the moment we believed in Jesus and confessed His name. This anointing is like the mantle Elijah had to do the great signs, wonders, and miracles testified about in the Scriptures. Because Elisha walked with Elijah, requesting a double portion of the anointing on Elijah, Elisha performed great signs, wonders, and miracles as well.

In the same way, God has designed His church to be full of fathers and leaders who anoint and pass down blessings and the anointing. The anointing is the enabling we are all seeking. The anointing is the dunamis power of God that does the heavy lifting and the impossible. The anointing is what makes the supernatural natural. In order to see the realities of Heaven come to earth we must have the anointing of Christ's Spirit operating in and through us. The prophet Isaiah declares in Isaiah 10:27 (NKJV), "It shall come to pass in that day that his burden will be taken away from your shoulder, and his yoke from your neck, and the yoke will be destroyed because of the anointing oil."

There are hardships in life that can only be lifted by supernatural intervention. The burdens and the yokes placed on us by the enemy can all by shattered through Jesus Christ. One reason why being in fellowship with other believers and attending a Spirit-filled church is important is the house of God is where we can go to get these yokes broken. Getting around other believers is how we can go to the next level in our walks with God. It is how we can become empowered to fulfill our purpose and our destiny. The spirit of the world wants to put a yoke (as opposed to a mantle from God) on you that is heavy. The Spirit of Christ has come to place a mantle of authority and victory on you that is light (Matthew 11:30).

The world says to look down here. Stay focused on this world and what you see in front of you. The Lord says to look up there. Focus on what is going on in Heaven. The Apostle Paul tells us Colossians 3:1-3 (NLT), "Since you have been raised to new life with Christ, set your sights on the realities of Heaven, where Christ sits in the place of honor at God's right hand. Think about the things of Heaven, not the things of earth. For you died to this life, and your real life is hidden with Christ in God." This world is not going to fulfill you. Jesus continually referenced Heaven and the truth He received from Heaven. Furthermore, Jesus came to testify that the deeds of this world are evil (John 7:7). If we are looking to this world to satisfy us, we are going to be greatly disappointed.

The Scriptures say that your life is "hidden". If your life is hidden then that means it needs to be discovered. Discovering exactly who you are in Christ is a lifelong journey. The Christian life is meant to be an adventurous, life-giving journey. Your identity in Christ goes far beyond just being saved and forgiven. When Elijah passed his mantle of authority onto Elisha, Elisha did not fully know what kind of prophet he was going to become. The miracles Elisha performed had yet to be discovered while he was still with Elijah. Not only did Elisha perform as many miracles as his predecessor, but he actually performed twice as many (as recorded in the Scriptures).

In the same way, you have yet to fully realize all of the great things you are going to do for God and His kingdom. True leaders want to see those they are leading thrive and prosper. Good parents want their children to go further in life than they did. When Elijah passed the mantle to Elisha, Elisha asked for a double portion. God honored this request, and Elisha performed twice as many miracles. Likewise, God originally designed the family and lineage of that family to grow greater with each passing generation.

The will of God for the generational line of your family is expressed plainly in Deuteronomy 7:9 (NLT), which says, "Understand, therefore, that the LORD your God is indeed God. He is the faithful God who keeps His covenant for a thousand generations and lavishes His unfailing love on those who love Him and obey His commands." One of the principles I have learned at church and by observation over the years is that the ceiling (or accomplishments) of one generation becomes the floor (or baseline) for the next generation.

As an example, think of a successful business started by the vision of one man. The man builds and builds the business. He then has children. As the business grows over time, the children grow older and begin to partake in the business. The children then have their own children. The business continues to grow, and before long the grandchildren are adults and now have ownership of a business that was established and grown long before they were ever born. The ceiling of the grandfather is now the floor of the grandchildren.

This is God's original intention for the family line. It is why King Solomon tells us in Proverbs 13:22 (NLT), "Good people leave an inheritance to their grandchildren, but the sinner's wealth passes to the godly." It is estimated that some 35% of Fortune 500 companies are family-controlled. This means that of the 500 largest US companies, over one in three are still primarily owned by the founder and/or their generational line (family). One reason we do not see more of this is because of generational sin. When sin and the adversary come in, what was meant for the next generation is lost.

The Scriptures say in Numbers 14:18 (NIV), "The LORD is slow to anger, abounding in love and forgiving sin and rebellion. Yet He does not leave the guilty unpunished; He punishes the children for the sin of the parents to the third and fourth generation." If Elisha had rebelled against Elijah, or given up on following him, then Elisha would have never received the double portion blessing and mantle of Elijah. Elisha would have missed his calling as a prophet, having never received the double portion mantle of Elijah to perform miracles.

The good news today is God can restore the generational line and the blessing. He can return what originally belonged to you. He has an inheritance, a double portion, for you to step into because of what Jesus did for you on the cross. You can be the great parent God has called you to be. You can be the end of the generational curse you never asked for growing up. You can be the beginning of a new generation that honors the Lord. Psalm 102:18 (NJKV) says, "This will be written for the generation to come, that a people yet to be created may praise the LORD."

The Word of God has been written for every generation. God's Word can help anyone triumph in this life, no matter what their upbringing. The key to seeing this kind of victory is by coming into agreement with what God says. We may not understand how God's Word can come true, but we can know that He is faithful to perform it. When we are struggling to believe things are going to work out, we can stand in faith on His promise in Romans 8:28 (ESV) which says, "And we know that for those who love God all things work together for good, for those who are called according to His purpose."

Rarely, if ever, does what God say to us match what we are seeing at the moment. This is why it is called faith. If we already saw what God promised then it would not require faith. Romans 8:24-25 (ESV) encourages us, "For in this hope we were saved. Now hope that is seen is not hope. For who hopes for what he sees? But if we hope for what we do not see, we wait for it with patience." As we wait on God to perform His Word and fulfill His promise, we wait expectantly. We exercise and train our spiritual muscles as we keep hope alive.

I believe when Elisha asked for a double portion from Elijah, he was demonstrating great faith. There had never been a prophet quite like Elijah in all of Israel's history. It took boldness for Elisha to ask his predecessor for increased anointing. Some might argue that Elisha was arrogant by asking his mentor for more, that it was prideful for Elisha to want twice as much as Elijah. However, when it comes to the things of God, we should be bold. We need to be forthright in receiving our inheritance from God.

The Apostle Paul tells the early church in 1 Corinthians 14:1 (ESV), "Pursue love, and earnestly desire the spiritual gifts, especially that you may prophesy." We should long for and pursue spiritual gifts. When Elisha asked for Elijah's mantle - asking him to make it double - Elisha was pursuing the spiritual gift. It's why God honored Elisha's bold request. Hebrews 11:6 (NKJV) says, "But without faith it is impossible to please Him, for he who comes to God must believe that He is, and that He is a rewarder of those who diligently seek Him."

Every believer in Christ has been given a mantle of faith. We have been given the authority to pass along this mantle of faith to others. Just as God used someone to lead us to Christ, we can lead others to this new life in Christ as well. Colossians 3:12 (NIV) tells us, "Therefore, as God's chosen people, holy and dearly loved, clothe yourselves with compassion, kindness, humility, gentleness and patience." These attributes of godliness can be cultivated and passed down from one generation to the next - from grandparent to parent, from parent to child, from child to grandchild.

For those who have messed up earthly families, God has given us each other, the body of Christ, to be our true spiritual family. Jesus tells His disciples (in front of his own earthly mother and brothers I might add) that the Kingdom of God is different from this world regarding family. Matthew 12:48-50 (NLT) says, "Jesus asked, 'Who is My mother? Who are My brothers?' Then He pointed to His disciples and said, 'Look, these are My mother and brothers. Anyone who does the will of My Father in heaven is My brother and sister and mother!'"

You have a family as one of God's children, and it is very big! You have brothers, sisters, fathers, and mothers all over the world who are seeking Christ just like you. You have a place where you belong. God has ordained the church for this very purpose. The purpose of the church is to provide support and to give believers a spiritual home where we can grow in our walks with Him and with each other. We were never meant to be alone as we seek God and pursue the things of His Kingdom. It is through spiritual fathers and mothers that we receive insight, wisdom, and new mantles of authority to go to the next level.

Jesus has passed the mantle of God's Kingdom to us. It is our responsibility to pass the mantle of God's Kingdom to others. This mantle represents authority. We are called to approach this life differently from the rest of the world. Jesus tells us in Matthew 6:31-33 (NKJV), "Therefore do not worry, saying, 'What shall we eat?' or 'What shall we drink?' or 'What shall we wear?' For after all these things the Gentiles seek. For your heavenly Father knows that you need all these things. But seek first the kingdom of God and His righteousness, and all these things shall be added to you."

As you seek God first, He may very well bring along a mentor. He may bring an "Elijah" into your life who wants to impart what they have onto you (and in a double portion, at that). The Lord has spiritual fathers and mothers throughout our churches who would love to minister to and raise up a new generation of believers. We see evidence of this every week in many churches, where busy parents and adults set aside time to minister to the youth. The sacrifices these spiritual fathers and mothers make are really a display of one generation passing the mantle of faith to the next generation.

I believe you are a part of the remnant in today's world. You are one of the faithful leaders who is passing the mantle along. Jesus says, "Freely you have received (the Kingdom of God), now freely give." (Matthew 10:8) Elisha never earned the double portion anointing from Elijah. He simply asked. In the same way, you cannot earn God's favor and anointing.

All you have to do is ask. Ask Him. Right now, wherever you are, open up your hands and ask God to give you the double portion.

Just as Elijah imparted a double portion to Elisha, I believe God is bringing others into your life for you to impart a blessing onto. You have freely received Christ. Now freely give all that He has to offer to others. The cloak of Christ you have been given is a cloak that multiplies. When you offer the cloak of Christ to another and they receive it, there are two cloaks instead of one. In God's Kingdom, passing the mantle means spreading the good news of God's Kingdom and watching God multiply the seed of His Word.

SCRIPTURE READING

2 Kings 2:9-14

Proverbs 13:22-24

Matthew 12:46-50

Romans 8:24-29

QUESTIONS TO ANSWER

A cloak, which is a piece of clothing, represents a position of authority. What are other physical objects you have seen that represent authority? *(For example: the crown of a king, regalia on a soldier, flags, etc.)*

Have you ever held a position of leadership? If so, did you have to find someone to replace you after your time of service was up?

Has anyone ever "passed the mantle" to you? *(For example: this could be a parent instilling values in you or a boss giving you more authority in the workplace.)* Did you feel empowered or overwhelmed when you stepped into this new position?

Chapter Seven
SPIRIT OF UNBELIEF

There are only two groups of people in the world regarding faith in Christ: those who believe and those who don't. On judgment day, every single person will have their eternal fate decided based upon whether they believed in Jesus or not. Jesus tells us in John 3:18 (ESV), "Whoever believes in Him is not condemned, but whoever does not believe is condemned already, because He has not believed in the name of the only Son of God." Whether or not we enter the Promised Land God has for us is based upon whether we believe or not. It is the test of our faith.

Hebrews 3:12-19 (NIV) tells us, "See to it, brothers and sisters, that none of you has a sinful, unbelieving heart that turns away from the living God. But encourage one another daily, as long as it is called 'Today,' so that none of you may be hardened by sin's deceitfulness. We have come to share in Christ, if indeed we hold our original conviction firmly to the very end. As has just been said: 'Today, if you hear His voice, do not harden your hearts as you did in the rebellion.' Who were they who heard and rebelled? Were they not all those Moses led out of Egypt? And with whom was He angry for forty years? Was it not with those who sinned, whose bodies perished in the wilderness? And to whom did God swear that they would never enter His rest if not to those who disobeyed? So we see that they were not able to enter, because of their unbelief."

The spirit of unbelief is one of the most destructive spirits there is. Unbelief is what hardens the heart. Unbelief is what prevents the miracle. Unbelief is the foothold the devil uses to deceive and lead astray. The good news today is there is an antidote, a cure, for unbelief: Faith. How do we take hold of this powerful medicine? This cure that stops the devil in his tracks? The Apostle Paul gives us the answer. He says in Romans 10:17 (NASB95), "So faith comes from hearing, and hearing by the word of Christ."

Hearing the Word of God is how we retrain and reprogram our thinking. God's Word shatters lies. Unbelieving thoughts and impure motives can all be dealt with when we take them before God and allow Him to shine His light on our hearts and minds. The Apostle Paul tells us in 2 Corinthians 10:4-5 (ESV), "For the weapons of our warfare are not of the flesh but have divine power to destroy strongholds. We destroy arguments and every lofty opinion raised against the knowledge of God, and take every thought captive to obey Christ."

When we recount and recall God's promises it stirs up our faith to believe again. Believing is what unlocks the spiritual door for the supernatural to manifest and happen in the world we live in and can see with the natural eye. When you believe, all things are possible (Mark 9:23). The enemy of our faith wants to rob us of knowing our identity in Christ. When we come to know who we are in Christ, we are powerful. We are no longer subject to the lies the devil is shooting at us. We can stop those flaming arrows by faith (Ephesians 6:16).

If the devil can get a person to stop believing, he can take away their power. Even Jesus did not perform very many miracles when around the spirit of unbelief. Mark 6:1-6 (NIV) says, "Jesus left there and went to His hometown, accompanied by His disciples. When the Sabbath came, He began to teach in the synagogue, and many who heard Him were amazed. 'Where did this man get these things?' they asked. 'What's this wisdom that has been given Him? What are these remarkable miracles He is performing? Isn't this the carpenter? Isn't this Mary's son and the brother of James, Joseph, Judas and Simon? Aren't His sisters here with us?' And they took offense at Him. Jesus said to them, 'A prophet is not without honor except in His own town, among His relatives and in His own home.' He could not do any miracles there, except lay His hands on a few sick people and heal them. He was amazed at their lack of faith. Then Jesus went around teaching from village to village."

Jesus didn't do many miracles in His hometown because of the spirit of unbelief. The idiom "familiarity breeds contempt" rings true in this passage of Scripture. The people who knew Jesus from a young age until He grew up had a hard time accepting Him as an authority figure and as the Son of God. In the same way, when God raises up people to lead or to a new level of greatness, we shouldn't be surprised when those most familiar with the person being promoted become more of an adversary and naysayer than an advocate.

Just as Jesus was rejected by His own hometown, the same can hold true for anyone seeking the Lord. Walking in the Spirit of Christ is going to cause you to shine. You are going to have a different spirit on you than the one people who used to know you are familiar with. You may still look the same physically on the outside, but the Holy Spirit inside of you is busy transforming you into a new person in Christ (2 Corinthians 5:17). When the Apostle Paul made the radical transition from being the persecutor of the early church to the spearhead promoter of the gospel, many people struggled with believing Saul the religious persecutor was now the biggest advocate for Christ.

The Lord can raise up whomever He so chooses. He can take a murderer and make them a preacher. He can take a preacher's kid and make them a pastor. He can take an orphan and make them a missionary. He can take a drug dealer and make them a leading business person who invests in the community and the church. There is no one too far gone that the arm of God cannot reach out and save. The one thing that will put a stop to deliverance and freedom is unbelief. The good news today is God knows the heart.

The Lord knows those who think they don't have the faith (but really they do), and those who claim to have the faith (but really they don't). 1 John 3:19-20 (ESV) tells us, "By this we shall know that we are of the truth and reassure our heart before Him; for whenever our heart condemns us, God is greater than our heart, and He knows everything." Unfortunately, we live in a world that tends to judge things by outward appearances instead of the heart of the matter. People take things in and make decisions based on what they see on the outside. However, God is quite the opposite. He sees the inside. He knows what's in the heart.

This is why it is so important as believers to listen to the Holy Spirit. It's why we are continually reading the Scriptures and studying the Word. We cannot just take life at face value. We cannot take whatever the pastor says as gospel with no personal knowledge of what the Bible says (even as much as we love our pastors and spiritual leaders). We must know the Word of God and make His Word the standard we measure all things against. Throughout my years of going through different seasons and different types of ministries, I have learned that what something looks like on the outside isn't always what is really going on.

The Pharisees looked great on the outside. They had mastered the art of playing religious. However, on the inside they were horrible (Luke 11:39-44). The spirit of unbelief loves to masquerade itself as pious and religious. Some of the biggest opponents to the ministry God has given me - the writing, the prophetic word ministry, and creating gospel media - have been those who have the spirit of religion on them. They have a spirit of unbelief. The way I know this is they love to argue. They are cynical, skeptical, and critical. They are modern-day Pharisees that need to be delivered from the spirit of unbelief.

When people refuse to believe in the power of the Holy Spirit, Jesus will go somewhere else to teach and use people who have willing hearts for God's work. Jesus doesn't care if you have a seminary degree or grew up in the church. Jesus cares about the heart. If you don't like the Holy Spirit, you don't like Him. The two are One. It is the Holy Spirit that gave us the Scriptures and yet people are denying the Holy Spirit and His power every day. As Jesus told the Pharisees, "You search the Scriptures because you think that in them you have eternal life; it is these that testify about Me; and you are unwilling to come to Me so that you may have life." (John 5:39-40 NASB95)

The promise God made to us and fulfilled is the Holy Spirit. Acts 2:32-33 (NLT) says, "God raised Jesus from the dead, and we are all witnesses of this. Now He is exalted to the place of highest honor in heaven, at God's right hand. And the Father, as He had promised, gave Him the Holy Spirit to pour out upon us, just as you see and hear today." Every time Jesus pours down the Holy Spirit on a church or group of people, the spirit of unbelief likes to go to work. A person gets supernaturally healed. Many people celebrate, but there are others who want to question. The Holy Spirit comes over a person, and they pray in tongues. Now the spirit of unbelief writes them off as a charismatic, because the spirit of unbelief says the gifts of the Holy Spirit are dead.

Just as Israel hardened their hearts in the wilderness, so too much of the church has hardened their hearts to the power of the Holy Spirit and the truth of the gospel. The reason? Unbelief. People have adopted the precepts of religious men instead of the truth of God. They have exchanged the power of God for manmade religion. For years I believed all of the Bible was true, and I still do. However, I wasn't raised knowing more about the gifts of the Holy Spirit as I now wish I had been. I knew I was eternally saved in Christ, but it wasn't until I was in college that someone came along and called me out as a "prophet".

At first, being told I was a "prophet" sounded really weird. Sure, I had always had visions and dreams. Some would say I had hyper-intuition. I would know things before they would happen or while they happened without a person telling me. I had the anointing of a prophet on me, but it wasn't until someone came along and called forth what I already was that I was made fully aware of this. Ephesians 4:11 tells us what the five offices of the real church are: apostles, prophets, evangelists, pastors, and teachers. Today I operate more fully in the prophetic because I have the knowledge of who I am in Christ. I am a prophet. I see in the Spirit with ease, and it's not because of anything I possess of myself but because of the grace God has given me.

As a prophet, I am constantly prophesying. There have been times when what I say offends people. As you can imagine, the spirit of unbelief is a big demon that likes to stop the words God has given me to speak. What I have learned as I've grown in the gift God has given me is that I don't have to defend what God gives me to speak. His Spirit defends what came from His Spirit through me. I always tell people when I'm ministering that when we are 100% yielded to the Holy Spirit, it is absolutely positively impossible for us to miss. The reason what we are saying is 100% true is because there is absolutely no lie or darkness at all in God. God is the Spirit.

The problems come when a person is only halfway yielded to God. They speak from what they think, spinning it as the word of God. People have been abused and hurt by misuse of the gift of prophecy. Unfortunately, the bad experience can be a breeding ground for the spirit of unbelief to come and make a home in. Skepticism and being slow to receive true prophecy can come over a person once they've been "burned" by false words. However, this does not nullify the office of the prophet in the church today, and it certainly does not nullify the gift of prophecy.

On the contrary, we all should be prophesying as the Spirit stirs in us. The Apostle Peter tells us, "Whoever speaks, is to do so as one who is speaking the utterances of God." (1 Peter 4:11 NASB95) The carnal nature is full of unbelief. The spiritual nature is full of faith. The spiritual nature is where our true power rests. When we understand the spiritual, the natural makes more sense. If we look at all the chaos and problems of the world, we might just say everyone has gone mad and is crazy. However, if we understand that we are living in the last days (1 John 2:18), that Satan is the prince of the air (Ephesians 2:2), and there is a massive spiritual war going on, the chaos and confusion we see makes more sense.

You can cultivate an attitude and atmosphere of faith in your home to keep unbelief from coming over your family, loved ones, and even church. When you are seeking the Lord, sharing what He is showing you, and keeping the praise music going, you are stirring up the Spirit not only in yourself but in your spouse, your children, your co-workers, your congregation, and your neighbor. Knowing that unbelief is what stops the flow of God's power should be an awareness we all have. If we can snuff out unbelief by making it a point to keep the word of God in our minds and hearts, then we are opening the door for the Lord to continue to show His power in fresh new ways.

Throughout the years I have had many book signings. I have traveled to different regions and cities, and one thing I have noted is that in certain places people are very hungry spiritually and want my books. They get really excited as they pass my table. Then I travel to other places, and there is a lack of interest. As a seer in the Spirit and someone who can sense what is going on in the spiritual atmosphere of where I am, I have noticed that in places that have a religious spirit, people yawn. They are not interested because they got it. They already know it all. There is a spirit that is blocking them from receiving what God has inspired me to write.

The religious leaders in Jesus' day had this same attitude. Churches and synagogues on every corner of the city. They grew up studying the Torah and the prophets. They got it. They already know it all. In John 7:45-52 (NIV) it says, "Finally the temple guards went back to the chief priests and the Pharisees, who asked them, 'Why didn't you bring Him in?' 'No one ever spoke the way this man does,' the guards replied. 'You mean He has deceived you also?' the Pharisees retorted. 'Have any of the rulers or of the Pharisees believed in Him? No! But this mob that knows nothing of the law—there is a curse on them.' Nicodemus, who had gone to Jesus earlier and who was one of their own number, asked, 'Does our law condemn a man without first hearing him to find out what he has been doing?' They replied, 'Are you from Galilee, too? Look into it, and you will find that a prophet does not come out of Galilee.'"

The good news today is I believe you are rising up above the naysayers and unbelief. Your confidence in the Lord is growing by the day. As you fix your mind and heart on what God can do, and not man, your faith is rising. As Psalm 118:8-9 (NKJV) declares, "It is better to trust in the LORD than to put confidence in man. It is better to trust in the LORD than to put confidence in princes." In Christ, you are a miracle worker (1 Corinthians 12:10). His Spirit lives and flows through you by faith.

The spirit of unbelief is being driven out of your home, workplace, and church. Your generational line is going to be a line full of believers. The spirit of unbelief will have no authority over your household. The Deuteronomy 1:11 thousandfold blessing is continuing through your family line because you are choosing to serve the Living God. You are saying yes to all that God has for you and your family. The counterfeit offers of this world and the unbelief are being driven out of your life by the Lord.

Today sing His praises! Lift up your voice in song and give thanks to the Lord for redeeming and saving you! God loves you, and He has big plans for you. He has unfathomable blessings that are going to pursue you and your loved ones for many years to come because of your willingness to surrender to Him. As the psalmist declares in Psalm 23:6 (NLT), "Surely Your goodness and unfailing love will pursue me all the days of my life, and I will live in the house of the LORD forever."

Your destiny is to spend eternity with the LORD. On this side of Heaven, God is speaking to you through the Spirit. The Lord is speaking to you through dreams and visions in the night (Job 33:14-15). He is increasing your faith to receive the spiritual blessings from Heaven through Jesus Christ (Ephesians 1:3). He is causing you to overcome all that the adversary has tried to sow in your life. You are rising higher and going to new levels of victory like never before.

SCRIPTURE READING

Psalm 118:5-14

Job 33:14-16

Mark 6:4-6

Hebrews 3:12-14

QUESTIONS TO ANSWER

What is an area of life or a difficult situation you are currently facing that seems impossible to overcome, and you are asking God to help you with?

How can you stir up your faith to conquer any unbelief and see a potential breakthrough? What is a Bible verse you can hold onto during this trial?

Who is a person you can commit to pray for in your life that you know needs Jesus and may have an unbelieving heart towards God?

Chapter Eight
DREAMERS LIKE JOSEPH

Greatness begins with a dream. Throughout the Scriptures, God continually sent dreams in order to instruct His servants and enlarge their vision. While every dream did not make sense at the time, God always fulfilled His word sent via dreams. Dreams are thoughts, events, images, and sensations occurring in the mind while one sleeps. Dreams are not limited to logic, because the one dreaming is asleep. Anything is possible in a dream. Dreams are a great place for faith to dwell and expand the mind. Perhaps it is one reason God loves to speak to His children through dreams.

Dreaming is how Joseph stepped into great power. He did not become the most powerful man in the world next to Pharaoh overnight. It started with a dream. The Scriptures say that Joseph was favored by his father Jacob more than all his other sons. Joseph was the firstborn of Jacob's one true love, Rachel. It should be no surprise that Jacob favored Joseph. Genesis 37:3-4 (ESV) tells us, "Now Israel loved Joseph more than any other of his sons, because he was the son of his old age. And he made him a robe of many colors. But when his brothers saw that their father loved him more than all his brothers, they hated him and could not speak peacefully to him."

Joseph had already ratted out his older brothers to his dad by giving a bad report about them while they were pasturing the flock. Dad favored his seventeen-year-old son more than the rest, making them jealous, so when God sends Joseph a dream it sends the older brothers into a conspiracy against him. Genesis 37:5-8 (NIV) says, "Joseph had a dream, and when he told it to his brothers, they hated him all the more. He said to them, 'Listen to this dream I had: We were binding sheaves of grain out in the field when suddenly my sheaf rose and stood upright, while your sheaves gathered around mine and bowed down to it.' His brothers said to him, 'Do you intend to reign over us? Will you actually rule us?' And they hated him all the more because of his dream and what he had said."

The second dream God sends Joseph causes the brothers to become even more indignant with him. Genesis 37:9-11 (NIV) tells us, "Then he had another dream, and he told it to his brothers. 'Listen,' he said, 'I had another dream, and this time the sun and moon and eleven stars were bowing down to me.' When he told his father as well as his brothers, his father rebuked him and said, 'What is this dream you had? Will your mother and I and your brothers actually come and bow down to the ground before you?' His brothers were jealous of him, but his father kept the matter in mind."

Whenever God sends us a dream, it can be offensive by its greatness. Greatness can cause offense not only to our own minds, but also to our own flesh and blood, our kinfolk. Familial competition and rivalry can be a source of great conflict and dissension. Jesus had issues with his siblings during his public ministry (John 7:5). Joseph's brothers were actually Joseph's biggest adversaries to his dream. However, God knew what He was doing. In His great wisdom, God used the brothers' jealousy to catapult Joseph into his destiny of greatness.

Dreaming big can get you in trouble. When I was wrapping up my undergrad and graduate degrees in college back home in Texas, I had great dreams for the next chapter of my life. A prophet actually gave a word to me that when I finished my education I would go to a coastal place to discover my destiny and purpose. What I didn't know is this word would cause both blessings and heartache. It was a two-edged sword of a word that would divide, destroy, and rebuild my life.

When Joseph received his word via dreams that he would one day rule over his parents and brothers, it was a two-edged sword. The word was true - but the word was also offensive. The same thing happened in my own life. The place God had me relocate to happened to be one of the most beautiful and influential cities in the world - Malibu, California. At the time, I was broke from six years of college yet had a mind full of ideas and big dreams. I also had a huge family, whom I loved, and who had strong opinions. Malibu offended some of those strongly opinionated family members.

People lashed out at me because I was pursuing the prophetic dream. Things were a little out of order. Likewise, Joseph was a little out of order when he disclosed his dream to his already envious brothers. It led to Joseph's pit. It led to Joseph being thrown into a pit, having his life spared by the persuasion of his brother Judah, and to Joseph being sold into slavery. Matters only got worse when Joseph's master, Potiphar, has a false accusation reported to him by his wife (who continually tried to seduce Joseph) that Joseph was trying to rape her. Joseph was then thrown into prison.

It took 13 long years for Joseph's dream to come to pass. It's worth mentioning, the manner in which Joseph had to wait all those years as a slave and prisoner was less than ideal. The Lord knew what He was doing all those years. God used Joseph's unfair situation to display His glory through Israel. It was from the prison in Egypt that God used Joseph's gift of dream interpretation to deliver him out of the prison and into his position as the most powerful man in Egypt next to Pharaoh.

The psalmist breaks down a beautiful picture of God using Joseph's life to do a marvelous work on behalf of His people. Psalm 105:16-23 (NLT) says, "He called for a famine on the land of Canaan, cutting off its food supply. Then He sent someone to Egypt ahead of them — Joseph, who was sold as a slave. They bruised his feet with fetters and placed his neck in an iron collar. Until the time came to fulfill his dreams, the Lord tested Joseph's character. Then Pharaoh sent for him and set him free; the ruler of the nation opened his prison door. Joseph was put in charge of all the king's household; he became ruler over all the king's possessions. He could instruct the king's aides as he pleased and teach the king's advisers. Then Israel arrived in Egypt; Jacob lived as a foreigner in the land of Ham."

In His foreknowledge, God sent Joseph to Egypt. He sent dreams to Joseph to prepare him for what was coming. In the same way, there are times when God will send you dreams to prepare you for what is coming. These dreams could be sent years in advance before the actual fulfillment of the dream so that when the time comes you will be better prepared, and the dream will make more sense. God loves to disclose Himself to those who belong to Him. Jesus tells us in John 14:21 (NASB95), "He who has My commandments and keeps them is the one who loves Me; and he who loves Me will be loved by My Father, and I will love him and will disclose Myself to him."

When Joseph finally reveals himself to his brothers thirteen years after they threw him into a pit, he tells them, "I am your brother Joseph, the one you sold into Egypt! And now, do not be distressed and do not be angry with yourselves for selling me here, because it was to save lives that God sent me ahead of you. For two years now there has been famine in the land, and for the next five years there will be no plowing and reaping. But God sent me ahead of you to preserve for you a remnant on earth and to save your lives by a great deliverance. So then, it was not you who sent me here, but God. He made me father to Pharaoh, lord of his entire household and ruler of all Egypt." (Genesis 45:4-8 NIV)

When bad things happen - people betray us, business goes south, a marriage goes south - God can still turn it around for the good. When Joseph was sold into slavery by his own brothers, God already knew how He was going to use the betrayal for the good. When I relocated to Malibu in my twenties, I went through several betrayals. I was a very heartbroken man before I got to thirty. What I didn't know was God was preparing me to become a writer. For years while in college I had seen pages, scripts, and books in the Spirit being written. At the time I supposed that I would become a writer when I got much older. I certainly didn't think I would become an author at age 29.

The amount of conflict and difficulty I grew up in still doesn't seem fair. However, I believe God was preparing me to become a writer through all of it. Writers are naturally full of internal conflict. It's what makes a writer a writer. A writer must hammer out on paper using words the internal struggle of emotions, desires, values, and interests that stand in the way of what they are hoping to achieve. Furthermore, the city full of more artists and writers than anywhere on earth with tremendous influence can be found in one place in particular: Los Angeles, California. LA is the film and entertainment capital of the world. The Hollywood dream birthed in me wasn't something that was by chance. It was a seed deposited by the Holy Spirit to prepare me for my destiny.

When Joseph rose to power in Egypt, he rose up to place in the greatest country on earth at the time. There was none next to Pharaoh and his Egyptian kingdom in all the world. The Lord used Joseph in a mighty way to preserve the generational line of Abraham, Isaac, and Jacob by sending him into the halls of power. It was through this lineage that the Messiah, the Savior of the whole world, was to be born over a millennium later. God is always thinking ahead. God is thinking in terms of generations. He is thinking far beyond what our minds can grasp or perceive (unless His Spirit reveals it to us).

The prophet Isaiah declares in Isaiah 55:8-11 (NASB95), "'For My thoughts are not your thoughts, nor are your ways My ways,' declares the Lord. 'For as the heavens are higher than the earth, so are My ways higher than your ways and My thoughts than your thoughts. For as the rain and the snow come down from heaven, and do not return there without watering the earth and making it bear and sprout, and furnishing seed to the sower and bread to the eater; so will My word be which goes forth from My mouth; it will not return to Me empty, without accomplishing what I desire, and without succeeding in the matter for which I sent it."

When God sent Joseph his dreams, He was thinking higher than what Joseph and his brothers were thinking at the time. When God sends you a dream, He is thinking much higher than what you may be thinking when He deposits that dream in your mind and heart. The important thing is to dream. Dreaming is an awesome experience when the Lord is in it. I tell people all the time to ask the Lord to send them dreams before they go to bed. One reason people don't dream as much as they would like or can't remember their dreams is because they aren't asking God to send them dreams (James 4:2).

Dreams can serve as a source of inspiration and motivation to rise higher and raise the bar of achievement in our lives. Because Joseph had powerful dreams as a teenager, dreams so provoking and unforgettable that they got him sold into slavery by his brothers, he still had hope while he sat in prison and waited for those dreams to be fulfilled. A shift happened for Joseph in the prison when the king's cupbearer and baker were thrown into confinement with him. God knew how he was going to use these two servants of the king so guess how He chooses to speak to them? That's right, a dream. Both servants have a dream, and Joseph has an interpretation.

Joseph rightly interprets the dreams. The cupbearer is restored to his place before Pharaoh, and the baker is executed (see Genesis 40). Unfortunately, the cupbearer forgets to tell Pharaoh about Joseph once he is set free. For two more years, Joseph had to sit and wait for his dream to come to pass. Have you ever had a dream, and it seems like it's about to happen - then all of a sudden, it doesn't? I have. In my twenties, for several months God spoke to me about going on a mission trip to Mozambique, Africa. I was having dreams and seeing African villages. A team from my church was going, and I felt led to go.

However, I was not able to go on the trip that summer. I was disappointed, but I had to lay the dream on the altar. Fast forward six months and a prayer team gave me a word about going to Africa. The dream and desire to go was resurrected. Long story short, over a year after the dream I was on an airplane flying to Maputo, Mozambique to work at one of Heidi Baker's Iris Ministries orphanages. There was a one-year delay in seeing the dream come true. The missionary trip to one of the poorest countries in the world changed my life forever. Seeing so much hope and gratitude amid great poverty changed the way I viewed life back home.

Friend, God is a man of His word. If He sends a dream, a vision, a prophetic word, or a Scripture, He is going to fulfill it. Our job isn't to make the dream happen. Our job is to believe while God works it into existence. When Joseph waited, he was powerless. He couldn't run to a friend's house and vent. He couldn't pick up the phone and call his pastor. He had no freedom. He was imprisoned. He had to depend on God whether he wanted to or not. Sometimes God will allow us to get to the lowest point, a place of complete impossibility, in order to demonstrate His power and His power alone.

The Lord is also instilling something immovable in our souls as we wait. Psalm 105:18 tells us that iron entered into Joseph's soul while in prison. Being falsely accused did something to him. It changed him permanently on the inside. The deep things of God are many times revealed in dreams. These revelations are what give us insight into the truth, and the truth is what brings us true freedom (John 8:32). Your sufferings are never in vain. Whatever God has purposed for your life will surely come to pass. Stay close to Him. Isaiah 14:24 (NIV) says, "The LORD Almighty has sworn, 'Surely, as I have planned, so it will be, and as I have purposed, so it will happen.'"

Joseph did not miss his destiny. Some would argue that it's Joseph's fault he sat in prison two more years for telling the cupbearer to remember him before Pharaoh, to get him out of his chains (Genesis 40:14-15) - that Joseph was looking to Pharaoh and not God to set him free. I believe Joseph wanted justice. He longed to be free. However, it wasn't time yet for Joseph to step into power. Two more years probably seemed like an eternity sitting in prison. However, two years in God's eyes is but a blink. The rest of Joseph's life would turn around in an instant when he got out. He would never go to prison again. His life would never be the same.

Maybe today you feel like you are in a prison of some sort. You are waiting for a dream to come to pass. Be encouraged. You may not have any way to change what is happening, but you do have God. He owns the timeline. Everyone and everything is subject to Him. Without Him, nothing would exist. If we will step back, reposition ourselves, and broaden our perspective by magnifying how great our God is, the challenge we are facing becomes minuscule next to Him. God can bend laws. He can break barriers and tear down walls. He even controls the human heart like a waterway in His hands (Proverbs 21:1).

The Lord sent Joseph ahead of Jacob his father in order to preserve the messianic generational line. God knew the end result from the beginning. In the same way, God already knows the end result of everything you encounter. A limited mindset that keeps us from rising higher to fulfill a dream can be broken by renewing our minds. The Apostle Paul tells us in Romans 12:2 (NIV), "Do not conform to the pattern of this world, but be transformed by the renewing of your mind. Then you will be able to test and approve what God's will is—His good, pleasing and perfect will."

Dwelling in the presence of God is where this transformation of the mind takes place. This is why going to church is powerful. Listening to worship music and singing His praises can redirect the entire ship of your life. Reading and listening to the Word of God can instruct you in the way to go (or not go). Joseph was a God-fearing man. He defeated the enemy when he fled temptation in Potiphar's house. He rightly interpreted dreams that landed him before Pharaoh because he wielded his spiritual gift of dream interpretation with precision and excellence.

Right now God is giving you a spirit of excellence to go along with the dreams He has for you. He is making you more productive and diligent like Joseph to take you and your family line further than you could ever imagine. His anointing is smoothing out those rough edges in your life. His oil is causing you to slip through the enemy lines and to see breakthroughs. Your victories are going to spill out as victory for others too (Romans 12:15). As you encourage others who may be in their "Joseph pit" time of need, you yourself are going to be encouraged. God is supplying all you are ever going to need in order to fulfill your God-given dreams (Philippians 4:19).

SCRIPTURE READING

Genesis 37:5-11

Psalm 105:16-23

John 14:20-23

Romans 12:14-15

QUESTIONS TO ANSWER

What is a dream you have had in the past that you believe is from the Lord?

Was that dream ever fulfilled? If so, does it make more sense why God sent the dream in advance to prepare you?

What is a big dream or vision you have for your life that you are praying God fulfills one day? Do you believe that if God, in all of His goodness, did it for Joseph, then He can do it for you too?

Chapter Nine
BREAKING BARRIERS

A barrier is defined as a fence or other obstacle that prevents access or movement from one place to another. It can be a circumstance that keeps people or things apart. It can also be something that prevents progress or communication. Barriers are what can block the way for us to move forward in life. When Jesus came to the earth, being revealed as the Messiah and the only true Son of God, He shattered the barrier between Heaven and Earth. The sin that separated mankind from God was dealt with when Jesus sacrificed Himself on the cross to make atonement.

To Jesus, your life is extremely valuable. If it wasn't, He wouldn't have suffered an excruciating, painful death for you. Your life is too important for you to not keep moving forward. Jesus is your barrier breaker. He is the new generational line maker. No matter what family you came from, who your earthly parents are, or what kind of childhood you had, you can rise above any barrier that has tried to limit you. You had no say as to when or where you would be born, or to what family you would be born into. You are more than just a product of your environment.

God has given you His Word and His Spirit to form and reform you from the inside out. The Bible is called the "living word" because it's the words of God that are so alive and that can radically transform any person's life. Hebrews 4:12 (ESV) tells us, "For the word of God is living and active, sharper than any two-edged sword, piercing to the division of soul and of spirit, of joints and of marrow, and discerning the thoughts and intentions of the heart." Whatever values you were raised to believe, whatever socioeconomic status you grew up with, whatever people you have grown up around, all of these things that have conditioned and formed you into who you are today are all subject to the Word of God.

I have seen both a poverty lifestyle and a prosperous lifestyle modeled before me, as well as experienced it for myself. I have seen people who were very talented never use their incredible gifts to do great things. I have also seen people who didn't have much use what little they had and accomplish seemingly impossible feats. I have learned over time that every single day we have a choice to make. Are we going to choose life, or are we going to choose our own way? Are we going to choose to work hard, or are we going to take it easy? Are we going to prepare for what's coming and do our best, or are we going to be careless and not make good use of our time God has given us?

Life boils down to choices. The choices you make today determine what kind of life you will have tomorrow. If you have grandparents who did well in life, who established a family, built their own business, and went to church, that's awesome; on the contrary, you might have parents who never could get their life together, and it took a toll on both them and their loved ones. That's unfortunate. Regardless of what family line you come from, it boils down to what you are going to do with the life in front of you. Blaming your problems on parents and grandparents is not going to help you rise higher and break generational barriers. You cannot dictate the past, but you can make good decisions for a better future.

The good news today is you can change the future by choosing to personally walk with God. When you make God's Word your standard to live by, you are choosing to walk by faith. You are choosing to agree with what God says, even if it contradicts what the world says. A person of faith believes before they see. In the Scriptures, one of the greatest barrier breakers we read about is David. David was the youngest brother of Jesse's eight sons. He was a shepherd in his youth and probably overlooked more times than not being the youngest sibling. If you feel overlooked by others, be encouraged. The greatest king of Israel in the Bible was too - even by the prophet Samuel and his own father!

When Samuel goes to anoint one of Jesse's sons to become the next king of Israel, he starts with the oldest. 1 Samuel 16:6-10 (NIV) says, "When they arrived, Samuel saw Eliab and thought, 'Surely the Lord's anointed stands here before the Lord.' But the Lord said to Samuel, 'Do not consider his appearance or his height, for I have rejected him. The Lord does not look at the things people look at. People look at the outward appearance, but the Lord looks at the heart.' Then Jesse called Abinadab and had him pass in front of Samuel. But Samuel said, 'The Lord has not chosen this one either.' Jesse then had Shammah pass by, but Samuel said, 'Nor has the Lord chosen this one.' Jesse had seven of his sons pass before Samuel, but Samuel said to him, 'The Lord has not chosen these.'"

If we stopped reading right here, we would consider the prophet's visit to Jesse's house a failed mission. None of Jesse's sons who were before Samuel had been chosen by God to be king. The oldest certainly looked by outward appearances to fit the bill to be a great king. If the general populace were to take a vote for the next king of Israel, they might have voted for Eliab, son of Jesse. However, what God had in mind for a leader versus what man had was very different. Man wants a solid resume. People want to see qualifications and strength.

1 Samuel 16:11-13 (NIV) goes on to say, "So he [Samuel] asked Jesse, 'Are these all the sons you have?' 'There is still the youngest,' Jesse answered. 'He is tending the sheep.' Samuel said, 'Send for him; we will not sit down until he arrives.' So he sent for him and had him brought in. He was glowing with health and had a fine appearance and handsome

features. Then the Lord said, 'Rise and anoint him; this is the one.' So Samuel took the horn of oil and anointed him in the presence of his brothers, and from that day on the Spirit of the Lord came powerfully upon David. Samuel then went to Ramah."

The reason David did not miss his great calling is because God made sure he would not be overlooked. Even when Samuel and David's father seemingly overlooked David (the youngest child) at first, God already had David marked to be the next king. In the same way, God is not going to miss or overlook you when He sends forth His servant to anoint you. You are not going to miss your call from God when you are doing your best to seek Him. The reason God chose David is because God knew David's heart. David wasn't perfect, but he had a heart set on pleasing the Lord.

When you set your mind and heart on Christ, you are like David. The anointing that blessed David and caused him to rise to royalty is going to be on you. Jesus is the reason you have access to this kind of promotion. The Scriptures say in Matthew 27:50-52 (NASB95), "And Jesus cried out again with a loud voice, and yielded up His spirit. And behold, the veil of the temple was torn in two from top to bottom; and the earth shook and the rocks were split. The tombs were opened, and many bodies of the saints who had fallen asleep were raised."

When Jesus took His last breath, His sacrifice immediately ended the separation between God's presence inside of the holy of holies at the temple and man outside the temple. His blood atoned for man's sin. The curtain of separation was a barrier keeping ordinary people who had sin from entering. Today that barrier of separation is gone through Jesus. We no longer have to make an animal sacrifice, or wait until Yom Kippur (the Day of Atonement) on the Hebrew calendar when the high priest goes into the holy of holies once a year, to have sin temporarily atoned. Instead, we have Jesus. We have full access to God's presence in Jesus' name.

Because the barrier caused by man's sin (the barrier being man separated from God because of sin - see Isaiah 59:2) has been destroyed by the Son of God, we can now move freely in Christ's Spirit to live the way God has called us to live. We don't have to fly out to Jerusalem to be a part of an animal sacrifice when we mess up. Jesus already took care of the sin. The key is we must come to Jesus to be forgiven and set free. Barriers are broken with God's power through Jesus.

Jesus demonstrated true power when He chose to die (Luke 22:42). He chose to obey the Father and give up His life so we could be given a better life (both now and in eternity). Death is compared to a seed in the Scriptures. Jesus says in John 12:24-26 (NIV), "Very truly I tell you, unless a kernel of wheat falls to the ground and dies, it remains only a single seed. But if it dies, it produces many seeds. Anyone who loves their life will lose it, while anyone who hates their life in this world will keep it for eternal life. Whoever serves Me must follow Me; and where I am, My servant also will be. My Father will honor the one who serves Me."

Jesus broke the most impossible barrier of death by offering up His life to God. Death has always been one inevitable thing guaranteed to all who are alive. When Jesus died sinless, His body couldn't stay dead. He was the perfect lamb of God (John 1:29). His literal earthly body would not decay because He is the Son of God and the Messiah (Psalm 16:10, Acts 2:29-32). Like a seed in the soil that has died, Jesus' body was buried in a tomb. On the third day, Jesus rose up from the grave, showing the world He had power over death. This is why the Bible says, "'O death, where is your victory? O death, where is your sting?' For sin is the sting that results in death, and the law gives sin its power. But thank God! He gives us victory over sin and death through our Lord Jesus Christ." (1 Corinthians 15:55-57 NLT)

When you choose to die to yourself, pick up your cross, and follow Jesus, you are breaking impossible barriers. Just as a seed doesn't produce more seeds unless it dies to itself, so we must die to ourselves in order to produce fruit that is pleasing to God. When you die to self and live to God, you have the Spirit of Christ in you that gives you His power to do the impossible. Barriers that have plagued you and your family for years - addictions, bad habits, poverty, divorce - all can be broken in the name of Jesus. A new generational line can be formed with God's help.

When David was taken from the last to the first, from the youngest child in the shepherd's field to the greatest ruler over all Israel, he was used as an example by God of what is possible when we seek the Lord like David did. David was chosen for his heart. Being the youngest, David probably always tried to keep up with his seven older brothers. Only God knew the desires of young David's heart. The Scriptures say that when a person delights themself in the Lord, He gives them the desires of their heart (Psalm 37:4). David had in his heart the ability to lead, win wars, and rule a nation. It was in a heart of worship that David did all these things and did them with excellence.

In the same way, when you delight yourself in the Lord, He is going to exalt you. The greatest and most rewarding commandment in the Scriptures is first found in Deuteronomy 6:5 (NIV), which says, "Love the LORD your God with all your heart and with all your soul and with all your strength." It is out of your love for the Lord that you are able to do things you never thought possible. It is from a place of love for God that you get breakthroughs and rise to new levels. The reason David won virtually every battle against his enemies is because he went to the Lord first.

While warring against the Philistines, David saw many victories because he sought the Lord first. 2 Samuel 5:18-20 (ESV) tells us, "Now the Philistines had come and spread out in the Valley of Rephaim. And David inquired of the LORD, 'Shall I go up against the Philistines? Will You give them into my hand?' And the LORD said to David, 'Go up, for

I will certainly give the Philistines into your hand.' And David came to Baal-perazim, and David defeated them there. And he said, 'The LORD has broken through my enemies before me like a breaking flood.' Therefore the name of that place is called Baal-perazim." Baal-perazim means "the Lord who breaks through".

The Hebrew word meaning "to break through" is parats. Parats can be translated into various words like prosperous, breaches, break down, break forth, broken through, destroyed, increased, overflow, and spread abroad. Maybe right now you need some breakthroughs in your life. The good news is you serve Baal-perazim, the Lord who breaks through. You can be the first person in your family to go to college. You can be the first family member to beat an alcohol addiction. You can be the one who breaks out of poverty and steps into prosperity and overflow.

When you believe in the Lord and trust in His word, then you can accomplish great things like King David. David did not step into power overnight. For years David had to struggle. He had to overcome being marginalized. He was chased down and hunted by King Saul. Even when he stepped into his role as king, he still had to battle. His own son Absalom sought to overthrow and destroy him. Following the Lord isn't always going to be easy, or even fun. However, it is the best path anyone could ever choose to take.

Psalm 16:11 (ESV) tells us, "You make known to me the path of life; in Your presence there is fullness of joy; at Your right hand are pleasures forevermore." True life can only be found in the One who created all things. John 14:5-6 (ESV) says, "Thomas said to Him, 'Lord, we do not know where You are going. How can we know the way?' Jesus said to him, 'I am the way, and the truth, and the life. No one comes to the Father except through Me.'" The only way to get the Creator, the Father of all, is through the Son.

Jesus is the answer to breaking barriers. He is the only one who can save us for all eternity.

He is the only one who can offer us living hope (1 Peter 1:3). You may have been born into unfair situations. You may even feel like you have been cursed at times. The good news is you are redefined the moment you believe in Jesus and confess His name. Your identity is wrapped up in and lived out by His Spirit that now dwells in you as one of God's children.

You are entitled to the blessings of your forefathers like Abraham, Isaac, and Jacob. Because you are in Christ, you are a part of the chosen. You are grafted into all of the magnificent promises of God (Romans 11:24). The anointing on you gives you the ability to overcome. The anointing on you heals your soul. The anointing on you causes you to catapult ahead in your calling. The odds may seem stacked against you, but those difficulties are no match for your God. God specializes in slaying giants and scaling mountains.

He brings peace in the chaos. He brings light and hope in darkness and confusion. He brings all you need at the exact time you need it. He is your Father. He greatly cares for you and deeply loves you. Jesus is the gate that is wide open to His sheep. The barrier between heaven and earth is no more for those who are in Christ. Jesus tells us in John 10:9 (NLT), "Yes, I am the gate. Those who come in through Me will be saved. They will come and go freely and will find good pastures." You have full access to the realities of Heaven while in this world. Jesus performed miracles, taught about mysteries from above, and knew where He was going all because He was from Heaven. He knew what was up there.

In the same way, you can know by the Holy Spirit some of these mysteries in Heaven now revealed. Jesus took on every infirmity, disease, generational curse, and all that is from the enemy so that you could be set free and have a better life. He took on poverty in order to make us rich. 2 Corinthians 8:9 (NKJV) says, "For you know the grace of our Lord Jesus Christ, that though He was rich, yet for your sakes He became poor, that you through His poverty might become rich."

Right now barriers holding you back are breaking. Yokes are breaking in Jesus' name. The poverty mindset and lack are being removed as you look to the resources of Heaven. Illness and diseases are being healed. Your soul is being refreshed and restored as the presence of the Lord fills your mind and heart. Your strength is growing stronger, and your vision is becoming clearer as seemingly immovable barriers break down and are destroyed by a flooding surge of God's power.

SCRIPTURE READING

1 Samuel 16:6-13

2 Samuel 5:17-20

John 10:7-11

John 12:24-26

QUESTIONS TO ANSWER

Are there limitations in your life that seem to keep you from fulfilling your calling/destiny?

Where do you need a "Baal Perazim", the Lord who breaks through, moment in your life?
(For example: financial breakthrough, debt paid off, disease healed, family member saved, etc.)

Do you believe that you can overcome the limitations, or barriers, that have been in your family line for years? What is a Scripture verse you can memorize to remind you that you can?

Chapter Ten
VISION OF THE BLACK MANTLE

While driving from one family gathering to another during the holidays not long ago, I was thinking and processing (as I usually do) all of the family dynamics. I love my family. God has blessed me with family (Ephesians 3:14-15). There are some wonderful blessings, talents, and attributes I have inherited from my ancestors. However, there are also some things that I have inherited that are not God's best. We all have traits, attributes, and generational blessings and curses that have been passed down to us, whether we want them or not.

The key to loving who we are and where we came from is to recognize both the blessings and the curses. God has not called us to bury our heads in the sand like an ostrich and pretend like nothing is wrong with our family. On the contrary, He wants us to deal with and even, at times, expose the problem. Not addressing issues is how generational curses can continue on to the next generation. This is why it is important to spend time with your children and be honest with them. When the time is right, and it's appropriate, tell them the truth of both the good and the bad in the family.

Let those you love know that we all have a choice. We can choose the good, and let go of the bad. We can embrace the family blessing and put a stop to the family curse. The Apostle Paul tells us in Romans 12:9-10 (NASB95), "Let love be without hypocrisy. Abhor what is evil; cling to what is good. Be devoted to one another in brotherly love; give preference to one another in honor." In other words, you get to choose what you hold close to your heart. Grab hold of what is good. Despise and stay away from what is evil.

While I was driving I was thinking of the good, the bad, and the ugly in my family. All of the sudden, I began to encounter a spiritual deep darkness come all over me and the car. I saw in the Spirt a huge black mantle draped over me and the car. This black mantle was a spiritual presence that had lingered over my family for generations. As I could strongly sense this darkness, it made me sad - even hopeless. However, as I continued to drive I began to see curses start flying off of me. The dark mantle representing family curses could not stick around.

I could see bursting light breaking through the darkness. It was a supernatural encounter that allowed me to see what the Apostle Peter says in 1 Peter 2:9 (NKJV): "But you are a chosen generation, a royal priesthood, a holy nation, His own special people, that you may proclaim the praises of Him who called you out of darkness into His marvelous light." God allowed me to see this black mantle to make a point and teach me a lesson. He was showing me that it did not matter what family I was born into, the truth is I have been born again into His family which is marvelous.

We all are born into sin and darkness of some form (see Psalm 51:5). Even the best of families have sin in the generational line - as the expression goes, every family has "skeletons in the closet". When we yoke ourselves to Jesus Christ and begin to walk with Him, carrying out what God has called us to do, worldly yokes and family bondages begin to break. Recently I woke up to a vision of a wooden yoke. I was trying to go along and do my work, but on this wooden yoke there was an engraving that said, "Man-made". The yoke seemed good, but it was a man-made yoke. It wasn't made by God.

Then I saw God shatter this yoke as I disassociated with it. I knew where that manufactured yoke was coming from, and it wasn't from Heaven. The yoke from Heaven is Jesus Christ. Jesus says in Matthew 11:28-30 (NIV), "Come to Me, all you who are weary and burdened, and I will give you rest. Take My yoke upon you and learn from Me, for I am gentle and humble in heart, and you will find rest for your souls. For My yoke is easy and My burden is light." The yoke of Jesus is not artificial or synthetic. It cannot be manufactured by men and man-made rules. I saw another yoke replace the wooden yoke. This yoke was light and powerful. It was the yoke of Christ.

Whether it's a black mantle or a wooden man-made yoke, we don't want it! We want Christ's mantle of authority and His yoke. People operating under a false mantle of legalism will make a person feel condemned and judged. They will make statements that tear down rather than edify. Throughout my life I have learned, sometimes the hard way, that there are spiritual "leaders" who are not who they may seem to be. I have had to shake off condemning statements and legalistic misused words - even using the Scriptures to do so - that caused my mind and soul great harm.

I have been around ministers who were so dominating and controlling that I couldn't even hear my own thoughts. Friends, these types of people are the ones we should steer clear of. The Apostle Paul warns us of these false ministers of light trying to place their heavy mantle on you, saying in Philippians 3:2-3 (BLB), "Beware of the dogs! Beware of the evil workers! Beware of the false circumcision! For we are the circumcision, those worshiping in the Spirit of God, and glorying in Christ Jesus, and not trusting in the flesh."

The prophet Ezekiel rebukes bad leadership through many of his prophecies in the Old Testament. The Lord speaks through Ezekiel, telling the shepherds of Israel that He is going to remove leaders who are not taking care of God's sheep. The prophet says to the leaders in Ezekiel 34:4 (NASB95), "Those who are sickly you have not strengthened, the diseased you have not healed, the broken you have not bound up, the scattered you have not brought back, nor have you sought for the lost; but with force and with severity you have dominated them."

Domination is not pleasing to the Lord, and He deals with people who are heavy-handed and dominating over others. One way we deal with and cope with being around dominating individuals is by developing strong boundaries. This is especially true when dealing with an overbearing relative or parent. While we love our family and those closest to us, it is important to have healthy boundaries - and even really strong boundaries when necessary. When we become an adult, the Lord wants us to act with more maturity than when we were younger. 1 Corinthians 13:11 (NKJV) tells us, "When I was a child, I spoke as a child, I understood as a child, I thought as a child; but when I became a man, I put away childish things."

We are not called to be yoked to man-made religion and rules that are not of God. We are not called to subject ourselves to overly domineering individuals. This is the issue Jesus had with the Pharisees and their overbearing teachings. As we are living in the last days, we are going to inevitably encounter modern-day scribes and Pharisees, who are overbearing and do not walk with Christ. They are full of rules and regulations, like the Pharisees. They make people feel condemned and "not good enough". This is not of Christ's Spirit. Christ enables and empowers as He rules and reigns. Overbearing leaders beat down and weigh down those they consider their "disciples" beneath them.

There are people today who are going around like the Pharisees did back in Jesus' time making converts, but it's not the true gospel. I like to call it "Jesus plus". They preach Jesus, plus some other stuff - rules, man-made ideology and theology, modern philosophy, etc. Jesus warns us of these types of dominating and deceptive people, just as He warned His disciples and condemned the Pharisees who traveled abroad proclaiming their message. Jesus declares in Matthew 23:15 (NASB95), "Woe to you, scribes and Pharisees, hypocrites, because you travel around on sea and land to make one proselyte; and when he becomes one, you make him twice as much a son of hell as yourselves."

The Bible warns us to be aware of adding to or taking away from the canon of Scripture. Moses instructs God's people in Deuteronomy 4:2 (NASB), "You shall not add to the word which I am commanding you, nor take away from it, so that you may keep the commandments of the LORD your God which I am commanding you." Again, in the final words of the entire Bible it says, "I warn everyone who hears the words of the prophecy of this book: if anyone adds to them, God will add to him the plagues described in this book, and if anyone takes away from the words of the book of this prophecy, God will take away his share in the tree of life and in the holy city, which are described in this book." (Revelation 22:18-19 ESV)

The good news is anyone can have a personal relationship with God. As individuals, we can know God on a level that keeps us from being misled. When we read the Bible and study the Word for ourselves, we can learn, grow, and know the Lord on an intimate, personal level. All believers should strive to grow closer to God so that we are spiritually mature. The Pharisees and the devil knew how to use the Scriptures to try and manipulate Jesus. Of course, it never worked. Jesus knew the Father, He knew the Word, and He knew His identity as the Son of God.

When you grow closer to the Father, the devil and those who are not of God will not be able to knock you off course. You know God personally. You have experienced His kindness. You know His divine character and His nature through both the written Word and by experiencing His presence. As the world grows colder and darker in the last days we are currently living in (see Matthew 24:12), you can keep the fire of God's love burning in you. You can be set apart from the course of this world. You are not going to be held accountable for what others have done, including your loved ones. You are going to be held accountable for yourself.

The prophet Ezekiel tells us in Ezekiel 18:1-4 (NCV), "The Lord spoke His word to me, saying: 'What do you mean by using this saying about the land of Israel: 'The parents have eaten sour grapes, and that caused the children to grind their teeth from the sour taste'? As surely as I live, says the Lord God, this is true: You will not use this saying in Israel anymore. Every living thing belongs to Me. The life of the parent is Mine, and the life of the child is Mine. The person who sins is the one who will die.'" In other words, the proverb says that the children are paying the price for their parent's bad behavior. The children are paying for the sins of the parents.

Ezekiel 18 goes on to say that the parent and the child will pay for their own sin. The child will not be responsible for the parent, and the parent will not be responsible for the child. For those who do what is right, whether the parent or the child, they will be blessed and live. For those who continue to do what is wrong, they will die in their own sin. When considering the generational blessings and curses in our family line, it is important to remember that everyone gets a choice. No matter what kind of family you come from, you decide whether or not you are going to honor the Lord and His Word.

For me, I had to choose to cast off the black mantle I saw in my vision. I had to keep driving. Keep moving forward. Keep running towards the blessings and promises of God. I have to choose to not look back. The Apostle Paul tells us in Hebrews 12:1 (BSB), "Therefore, since we are surrounded by such a great cloud of witnesses, let us throw off every encumbrance and the sin that so easily entangles, and let us run with endurance the race set out for us." The reason I am able to rise above addictions in the family line, to beat poverty, and to have a sound mind is because I am choosing to fix my eyes on the Lord and run. As I run, I am throwing off the sins that have held back my family line. I am choosing what God says.

The same is true for you. Hebrews 12:2 (BSB) says, "Let us fix our eyes on Jesus, the author and perfecter of our faith, who for the joy set before Him endured the cross, scorning its shame, and sat down at the right hand of the throne of God." Where you fix your eyes is where you are going to gravitate towards. Friend, fix your eyes on Jesus. This is how you throw off those snares that have held you back. It's how spiritually black mantles are cast off.

You have the authority to make a change. You don't have to accept the way things are. Jesus did not accept the religious leaders' traditions because they were wrong. He set a new standard and a new way of life. Jesus taught the way of grace and peace. He taught truth. Violence ended with Him (Isaiah 42:3). Healing began with Him. Your healing begins with Jesus. Like a bruised reed, the deep injuries beneath the surface can only be healed by Christ.

When you don't know what to pray, God does. Romans 8:26 (ESV) tells us, "Likewise the Spirit helps us in our weakness. For we do not know what to pray for as we ought, but the Spirit Himself intercedes for us with groanings too deep for words." As a believer, you have been given Christ's Spirit. His Spirit intercedes for you. His Spirit advocates on your behalf. His Spirit empowers you to rise above darkness and step into His light. You do not have to accept the wrong mantle. Just as Jesus did not accept the teachings of the religious leaders of His day, just as He chose to go against the grain, even at the expense of His life, so you can choose to not accept what was handed down to you.

With Christ's Spirit dwelling in you, you can do all things (Philippians 4:13). Divorce may run rampant in your family. Hereditary disease may have taken the lives of family members in the past. Addictions and bad habits may have plagued those who have gone before you. However, that does not have to be you. Your strength and your will alone cannot stop it. What can stop it is your faith. What stops the dark mantle is your agreement with God's Word and trust. Your demons are not your demons. They are the devil's. They don't belong to you. They no longer have a right to your life.

The Spirit of God kicks these fowl spirits out (Matthew 12:28). Right now I believe spiritual strongholds are breaking in your life. Christ in you is being formed (Galatians 4:19). You are a new creation in Christ, a wonderful masterpiece of God's working (2 Corinthians 5:17). The old things are beginning to fall away as the newness of life comes forth. Sobriety, faithfulness, health, healing, prosperity, love, and joy are the new standards in your family. All of them are yours because of what Christ did for us.

Right now God is bringing you to a place of trust. Your cares are being put to rest as you center your hopes and dreams on your Creator. Jeremiah 17:7-8 (NLT) encourages us, "But blessed are those who trust in the LORD and have made the LORD their hope and confidence. They are like trees planted along a riverbank, with roots that reach deep into the water. Such trees are not bothered by the heat or worried by long months of drought. Their leaves stay green, and they never stop producing fruit." Your roots are going deep into the water of God's Word beneath the surface of this world.

You are living from the inside out. Yokes are breaking. Healthy boundaries are being established. God has given you His shield of victory, and His help has made you great. He has made a wide path for your feet to keep you from slipping (2 Samuel 22:36-37). The Lord is moving the wrong people from your life and bringing the right people across your path. Anointings are being released causing things to fall into place. As you press onward in faith, you are like King David as he forged ahead into battle. The angels of God are moving on your behalf to bring the victory.

Generational roots of blessing and favor are growing your family tree strong. Betrayal, heartache, and disappointment are not going to keep you from becoming who God made you to be. On the contrary, God is using the setbacks and pullbacks to catapult you to the next level of your destiny. With the Lord's help, you are unstoppable. You have not missed your divine assignment. Your calling is not lost. God is completing the good work He has started in you (Philippians 1:6).

SCRIPTURE READING

Deuteronomy 4:1-4

Ezekiel 18:1-4

Philippians 3:1-3

Revelation 22:16-19

QUESTIONS TO ANSWER

Are there any family curses, or a "black mantle", in your family line that you are praying God cuts off from yourself and your family line? What are some of them specifically you can ask God to remove?

Are there any man-made yokes of religion that need to be broken from your life or your loved ones' lives? If so, what are they?

Do you fully trust God? Are there any areas of struggle you are having a hard time letting go of for God to deal with?

Part Three

CREATE

*"For we are God's handiwork, created in Christ Jesus to do good works,
which God prepared in advance for us to do."*
Ephesians 2:10

Chapter Eleven
STARTING OVER

In life there are seasons we go through that require starting over. The phrase "nothing lasts forever" is a reminder that we are living in a world that is always changing. What we know, see, and feel is continually evolving. While change can be good or bad, we have to be ready in and out of season to do what God has called us to do (2 Timothy 4:2). In my own life I have been through various seasons where I've had to hit the reset button. Things came to an end, sometimes unexpectedly. Other things ran their course, and it was time to move on.

In my twenties, I was finishing up college at the exact same time as the greatest financial crisis of the century. The Global Financial Crisis of 2007-2008 was not the ideal time to be getting out of college and looking for a job. A bursting housing bubble market and major banks collapsing (like the Lehman Brothers) triggered a global financial shockwave. The Great Recession characterized by high unemployment and economic hardship was one of the most severe economic downturns since the Great Depression.
When I finished my bachelor's degree in business in 2008 and my Master of Business Administration in 2009, I was being released into a world of financial distress.

Like almost everyone else, the financial crisis took its toll on my personal life. I spent much of my twenties acquiring and then slowly losing all I had attempted to acquire financially. I was in financial ruin by the time I finished living out my twenties. I was bankrupt with destroyed credit and loans. Ever been there? Not fun. I had to build my life from the ground up. My life looked like ground zero. The aftermath of all my hard work looked like ash. For a while, all hope was lost.

The best advice and the greatest turning point came when one of my parents said to me, "Take life one day at a time. When anyone asks you what you are doing, you tell them you are taking things one day at a time." This token of wisdom was the groundwork for what was to come. Jesus tells us in Matthew 6:34 (NLT), "So don't worry about tomorrow, for tomorrow will bring its own worries. Today's trouble is enough for today." When I began to adopt this "one day at a time" mindset, I began to make better decisions. I was not planning for retirement. I was not trying to figure out how to make everything work. My life had been destroyed. It was a mess.

Starting over meant I had to focus on whatever was in front of me that day. Looking into the future was almost impossible. There was still smoke and ash for miles, and I could not see any way out or how to move forward. However, I heeded my parent's advice and adopted another motto: "Choose life." As I began to make decisions - some easy, some difficult - I would choose decisions that added life or value. The inspiration for this motto comes from Deuteronomy 30:19 (NIV) which says, "This day I call the heavens and the earth as witnesses against you that I have set before you life and death, blessings and curses. Now choose life, so that you and your children may live."

As I began to make better life-giving decisions, naturally my life began to get better. Things were still far from perfect, but the ship was starting to move in the right direction. As I started studying the Bible again, I spent almost an entire year reading the Bible cover to cover. I took five journals of notes and committed to spending time with God every single day no matter what. At the time I was not working, but the personal sabbatical altered my life forever. About the time I was finishing reading the Bible, God stirred my spirit up to not only dream again but to start doing what I had dreamed about doing in the past.

While listening to a friend play the piano one day, a voice (the Holy Spirit) told me it was time to write my first book. I had attempted to write in the past, but I had never had the resolve or attention span to actually write a whole book. This time it was different. I sat down and began to type on the computer. Floods of ideas and the structure for a book came to mind. By the end of the day, I had the blueprints for writing a devotion book full of encouragement to live by faith. The inspiration was from my own experience of taking life by faith one day at a time. Today my readers know this book, Tasting the Goodness of God: 31 Daily Devotional for Everyday Living.

Tasting the Goodness of God became the cornerstone and beginning of a worldwide, multimedia ministry based upon personally experiencing the goodness of God. MLM Publishing was birthed in response to needing to publish my new book. Shortly after publishing the new book, I returned to work at the family business back home. When I wasn't working, I was on the road hosting book signings. Starting my life over at age 29 was not easy. It took a lot of hutzpah to launch into book writing and to begin tackling a financial mess.

At first, it seemed like I was scaling an impossible mountain. The steps were small, and the journey was far. However, God reminded me what He reminds all His people: "Do not despise these small beginnings, for the LORD rejoices to see the work begin." (Zechariah 4:10 NLT) Starting over takes guts. It requires faith. One of the most notable characters in the Scriptures who had to start over is Job. Job was extremely wealthy. He had a quiver full of children. He was a blameless man who did right by others. When Satan is allowed to take away all that Job possesses (Job 1:12), Job's life is completely destroyed. All of his children are killed, his possessions are taken away, and his wife tells him he should just curse God and die (Job 2:9).

After being brought to ruin, Job loses his health. Furthermore, his own friends give him poor counsel and do nothing to help the situation. If the Bible has one book that defines hitting rock bottom, it is the Book of Job. Job had every reason to be bitter, to lose hope, to give up, and an opportunity to turn away from God. Job chose to stay in faith. He did not abandon his walk with God. In the same way, there are times when it seems like the mishaps and misfortunes around us are overwhelming. It can feel like there is no way out. The good news is there may be no way of escape, but there is always a way to rise above and overcome.

When we move over into the realm of faith, we are no longer focused on the situation. We are focused on who God is and what He can do. Job did not suffer forever. After being corrected and addressed by the Lord, Job says to Him in Job 42:2 (ESV), "I know that You can do all things, and that no purpose of Yours can be thwarted." The reason Job survived the complete annihilation of his life brought on by Satan is because Job knew His God. Starting over was not impossible, because Job was passing the test. He held onto the Lord. Job's wife and his friends gave bad counsel throughout Job's great trial, and yet he still was able to rise above the turmoil and bless the Lord (Job 1:21).

In the end, God caused Job to prosper greatly. The Lord gave Job double for his trouble. Job had ten more children. His possessions were twice what they were before. He lived to see four generations of his family. (Job 42:10-17) Job's life story is a testimony for us all. It is an encouragement that God can restore anyone's life. He can restore a broken, or even completely destroyed, family lineage. God's grace is abundant. Creating new life is God's specialty. He gives life to the dead (Romans 4:17). When God speaks, things that were not come into existence.

God is the Creator, and we are His creators made in His image. Our gifts, talents, and abilities are all bestowed upon us from above in order to do good works. Creativity is built into the heart of everyone. A few days ago I was driving home, and I began to have a vision. In this vision, I saw all these jars floating in the sky. The jars were full of potential. The jars represented all the different gifts and talents God had put inside of them. Then I saw angels come out of Heaven and begin to take the lid off of these jars. All of what was contained began to come forth out of the jars and spread. At the time I was having the vision I was seeing a lot of breakthroughs in my own life.

God was showing me that He was taking the lid off in my life. He was unlocking stored-up potential and turning potential success into reality. The same is true for you. Right now I believe angels are taking the lid off in your life. Those jars of talent buried in your soul are coming up. The lids are being removed so you can go higher and further than you ever thought possible. Everyone is loaded with great potential because we are all made by a great God. When God tells us we are made in His image, that is not a thing to take lightly. Do you know who God is? He is the All-Powerful, the great I AM.

No matter what you have been through or what you are going through, God is still right there beside you. Fighting through a nasty divorce, losing a job, filing for bankruptcy, suffering through a church split, betrayal, health problems - all of these unfortunate events can lead us to the end of a path we were once on. Some people get stuck at the end of the road and never move on. Bitterness sets in. Hopelessness and despair take root. This is where our faith is tested. Will we rise above the devastation and hold fast to the Lord, believing He can start a new path of life to travel on?

Reading and holding onto the Word of God is how we defeat the enemy and work through tribulation. When I lost everything - houses, a car, credit, relationships, my mental health - I had to choose to trust what God said. The way I started over was by reading the Bible and clinging to His Word. The prophet Isaiah declares in Isaiah 48:17 (NKJV), "Thus says the LORD, your Redeemer, The Holy One of Israel: 'I am the LORD your God, Who teaches you to profit, Who leads you by the way you should go.'"

The promises of God are absolutely remarkable. They are miraculous and powerful. One Scripture can totally transform your life when you grab hold of it. To this day there are different Scriptures that I speak and remind myself of as I go about what I'm called to do. When business is slow, I remind myself what God said: "I am the head and not the tail. The Lord is showing me the way to prosper. As the righteous in Christ, I am rewarded with prosperity." When I am struggling with my health, I remind myself of God the Healer: "The Lord is Jehovah Rapha, my Healer. He is causing me to prosper and be in good health. He heals all my diseases."

The Bible is your weapon for fighting the spiritual war we are in. Friends, we are living in the last days. The spiritual warfare is only going to intensify as we approach the coming of the Lord Jesus. There are divine assignments God has ordained for you to complete. No one is exempt from participating. A Christian's work is never finished. No matter how much wealth you accumulate or what obstacles you overcome, there is always something every believer has been called to do for every season they are in. Many people have been trained to just "make it to retirement" and you've made it to life's finish line - or by chance hit the jackpot, that somehow by becoming wealthier overnight everything is going to be fixed.

Nothing could be further from the truth. More power comes with more responsibility. Jesus warns us in Mark 4:18-19 (NLT), "The seed that fell among the thorns represents others who hear God's word, but all too quickly the message is crowded out by the worries of this life, the lure of wealth, and the desire for other things, so no fruit is produced." Again, Jesus says in Luke 12:48 (NLT), "When someone has been given much, much will be required in return; and when someone has been entrusted with much, even more will be required." The material things of this world are not going to satisfy you.

The number one cause of divorce is lack of commitment. Just as a husband and wife are in the most holy covenant of commitment, a "till death do us part" agreement, so every believer is in a covenant with God. Commitment has become more and more uncommon these days. Loyalty and trust have flown out the window, along with Christian values, in today's culture. Infidelity, financial hardships, physical and/or emotional abuse, previous marriage baggage, and a lack of honesty can all contribute to marital commitments coming to an end. While divorce is horrible, and God tells us He hates divorce (Malachi 2:16), there are other things the Lord abhors as well.

Walking away from destructive situations, whether it be a marriage, an unhealthy job or relationship, or a harmful ministry or church, is going to require starting over. The longer one has been in a situation, the harder it may be to walk away and start over at first. However, God is always for setting people free, breaking yokes, and alleviating hardships. We are called to help in this matter. That's why the proverb says in Proverbs 3:27 (ESV), "Do not withhold good from those to whom it is due, when it is in your power to do it."

Putting and keeping God first is how we start over. Turn the page and begin a new chapter. Just make sure you invite the Holy Spirit to lead you going forward. His Spirit is your guide. You and He are in a spiritual partnership that is between you and Him. Your life is full of blank canvases. You may or may not be a literal artist, but God gives us a clean canvas every day to start painting a new picture. He gives us tools and resources on a daily basis to help us keep building. You have the ability to build all over again from scratch. Lamentations 3:22-23 (NLT) tells us, "The faithful love of the LORD never ends! His mercies never cease. Great is His faithfulness; His mercies begin afresh each morning."

The reset button starts every single day. If you are really struggling, the reset button may be every hour. God establishes us, and He can reestablish us when we need to move over or make life adjustments. 1 John 1:7 (BSB) says, "But if we walk in the light as He is in the light, we have fellowship with one another, and the blood of Jesus His Son cleanses us from all sin." The blood of Jesus is what purifies our minds and hearts. The blood of Jesus is how we can start a new beginning. In God's eyes, the blood of Jesus makes atonement for all of our sins, shortcomings, and mistakes.

This is why we celebrate and worship Jesus Christ, the Son of God. He is the reason anyone has true and lasting hope. The thorns and thistles of this world are not going to keep you from your destiny. You have a Helper to lead you where you should go. The gentle voice of the Holy Spirit will speak to you when you get quiet and listen to His counsel. The psalmist declares in Psalm 51:7-11 (NCV), "Take away my sin, and I will be clean. Wash me, and I will be whiter than snow. Make me hear sounds of joy and gladness; let the bones You crushed be happy again. Turn Your face from my sins and wipe out all my guilt. Create in me a pure heart, God, and make my spirit right again. Do not send me away from You or take Your Holy Spirit away from me."

Only the blood of Jesus can permanently expunge our sins and iniquities. Only the blood of Jesus can destroy the family curses that have plagued us for so many generations. Only the blood of Jesus can purify us from the inside out. It is God, and only Him, who can create a clean heart. We all are full of darkness until we come to know Him and His marvelous light. He is our lighthouse leading us to safety. Starting over means we need to first turn the light on so we can see more clearly.

Mistakes of the past can create wisdom we did not have before. Repeating those mistakes can be avoided when we choose to follow His light. Psalm 119:103-105 (NIV) encourages us, "How sweet are Your words to my taste, sweeter than honey to my mouth! I gain understanding from Your precepts; therefore I hate every wrong path. Your word is a lamp for my feet, a light on my path." The path you are looking for can only be found in Him. Trust Him. He will never mislead you.

When someone asks you what your plan for life is, your answer is, "God." God is the plan. He has you in His hands. Only He knows what tomorrow holds. You are living for Him, and it is His word that sustains you (Jeremiah 15:16). You are in covenant with your Maker. You are never alone. You and He are in partnership, an unbreakable bond that is fireproof and divorce-proof. You are committed to Him, and He is fully committed to you. By spending time with Him in prayer and in reading His word, you are investing in this glorious future you have with your heavenly Father.

SCRIPTURE READING

Job 42:10-17

Isaiah 48:15-19

Matthew 6:31-34

Mark 4:18-20

QUESTIONS TO ANSWER

When is a moment in time that you had to hit the reset button? *(For example: after fighting with a spouse, child, or parent; starting a new job; finishing school; going through a divorce, etc.)*

Looking back can you see the grace of God helping you through the difficult time?

Is there an area of life you would like to start over that you would like God to help you with? *(For example: getting married, starting a new job, restoring a relationship, moving, spending more time with God, etc.)*

Chapter Twelve
YOUR PRAYER LIFE

Recently I was talking to a little boy about his day at school. Through his rimmed glasses and fresh school haircut this sweet child followed me around at work telling me with excitement about the treasure box at school. He got to pick out his favorite candy as a reward. I gathered from listening and my memories of attending the same elementary school that the teacher would recompense good behavior and celebratory moments by allowing the young students to pick a treat from the treasure chest.

The boy was energized as he relived the excitement of the day. I had seen the same boy a few days before, and he was tired and could barely stay awake. The contrast of the two days was stark. He was like a different child. While we all smile and are amused by the vibrant personalities of little kids, the truth is in some ways we don't change much as we become older. Like with this kid, we have good days and bad days. Some days we are more excited and hopeful than others. When Jesus taught about the Kingdom of God, He always welcomed little children.

Little children set the example of how we should be as we step into God's Kingdom and learn about the ways of God. Jesus tells us in Matthew 18:1-6 (NASB95), "At that time the disciples came to Jesus and said, 'Who then is greatest in the kingdom of heaven?' And He called a child to Himself and set him before them, and said, 'Truly I say to you, unless you are converted and become like children, you will not enter the kingdom of heaven. Whoever then humbles himself as this child, he is the greatest in the kingdom of heaven. And whoever receives one such child in My name receives Me; but whoever causes one of these little ones who believe in Me to stumble, it would be better for him to have a heavy millstone hung around his neck, and to be drowned in the depth of the sea."

Jesus is adamant about being careful and loving around children. Children are the innocent ones of the world. Their minds were made by God to be sponges. Their hearts are tender, and anyone who misleads one of God's little ones is destined for serious trouble. In the same way, God considers us His children. Even if you are eighteen years or older, you are still a child in God's eyes. The Apostle John calls believers "little children" nine times in his first epistle. Is John just talking to the kindergartners? No. He is addressing the early church. He is addressing us.

Buried inside of you is a treasure chest. It is loaded with dreams, ideas, creativity, and talent. It is a mystery until it is drawn up and out into the open. Jesus tells us in Matthew 12:34-35 (ESV), "For out of the abundance of the heart the mouth speaks. The good person out of his good treasure brings forth good, and the evil person out of his evil treasure brings forth evil." Whatever is buried deep down in the heart of man, this is what is going to come out as it begins to overflow. This is why Solomon tells us in Proverbs 4:23 (NIV), "Above all else, guard your heart, for everything you do flows from it."

Your prayer life is where your heart is conditioned to do what is right. Prayer is where real change begins. Not only is prayer how you communicate directly to God the Father, it is also how you draw out the treasures in your heart. The deep desires planted, hidden, and protected in the soil of your heart can be grown and come to the surface through your prayer life. Your talents, gifts, and calling must be drawn out by the Holy Spirit and God's Word. The prayer room is where things are created and formed. Not only is talking to the

Lord when we discover desires in our hearts, but it is also how we get things off our chest and blow off steam.

In this life, there is going to be stress. There are going to be problems. This is why people often "vent" to other friends. They let out steam. The best person you can ever vent to is Jesus. Talking to Jesus like your closest friend is prayer. Jesus has been through all that we have, and yet He still knows a better way. That is what makes Him (or should) our very best friend. Hebrews 4:15-16 (BSB) says, "For we do not have a high priest who is unable to sympathize with our weaknesses, but we have one who was tempted in every way that we are, yet was without sin. Let us then approach the throne of grace with confidence, so that we may receive mercy and find grace to help us in our time of need."

The Lord wants us to be honest and true with Him. He does not expect you to act pious and put on a religious show for Him when you pray. As a matter of fact, the Pharisees got in trouble for this very thing. Jesus instructs us in Matthew 6:5-6 (NKJV), "And when you pray, you shall not be like the hypocrites. For they love to pray standing in the synagogues and on the corners of the streets, that they may be seen by men. Assuredly, I say to you, they have their reward. But you, when you pray, go into your room, and when you have shut your door, pray to your Father who is in the secret place; and your Father who sees in secret will reward you openly."

The secret place is limitless. The secret place is where you and the Father commune. It is the place of tremendous power. God has spoken to people for generations through the prayer room. Men and women have risen to power publicly by having a private prayer life. Your prayer life is where you go to war. It is where angels are put on divine assignment to carry out what is spoken and revealed. Your prayer life is the solution to life's problems. Praying for wayward children, calling out for financial provision, asking for supernatural healing, seeking counsel from above - all of these things and more happen in the prayer closet.

Many of the biggest milestones in my life have come after something was first revealed in my alone time with God. I knew for seven years I would one day become a writer. Every day I would see pages and pages being written in the Spirit. However, this revelation did not become reality overnight. It took years before I finally became a published author. I have learned over the years that God prepares us years in advance for what's coming. Sometimes God will do things seemingly overnight. Other times it takes months, and even years, before a revelation from the Spirit in the prayer room is fulfilled. However, these revelatory moments can motivate us to keep moving forward and to have hope for what's coming.

For believers, walking around praying should be normal. We may not be sitting still praying out loud alone in the prayer room for hours at a time, but we can be praying under our breath or have thoughts of prayer running through our minds as we go about our day. This is what it means to "pray without ceasing" (1 Thessalonians 5:17). The Lord knows we have jobs and responsibilities. He knows we have tasks to accomplish. However, He wants you to take Him with you as you go.

Recently I was on the phone talking to someone who was going on and on about an issue they were having. I knew they were frustrated, but I knew the issue shouldn't be so difficult to fix. After I hung up the phone, immediately I heard the Lord say, "Poverty spirit." These two simple words gave me insight into the problem. The issue this person was having stemmed from a poverty spirit. The issue itself was being blown out of proportion and made difficult to resolve because of this particular spirit.

This revelation came from the spirit of counsel (see Isaiah 11:2), that is, the Holy Spirit. When you have an active prayer life, the Spirit of God will talk back to you. He will counsel you. He will tell you things you wouldn't have known otherwise. He will shed light on the darkness. Having an active prayer life is one way to turn the light on and keep it on. Jesus tells us in John 8:12 (NASB95), "I am the Light of the world; he who follows Me will not walk in the darkness, but will have the Light of life."

Unfortunately, there is so much darkness that has been passed from one generation to the next. Adults are people who were once children. The values adults were taught as children and shown by the actions of their family members cause them to have a strong propensity to carry out that same behavior. We see this all the time. A parent is an alcoholic and lives for the drink. The kid grows up and lives at the bar. A parent deals with depression. The kid grows up and struggles with the same shadowy feeling. The list of issues is long and stems from generational darkness that needs to come to light.

The only way to break this vicious family cycle is the light of Jesus. When you have Jesus, He shows you things. He helps you deal with pain and issues you may have no control over. The closer you get to Christ in the prayer room, the more mysteries He will reveal. Intimacy through prayer with Jesus Christ is how the heart heals and grows. I have been through tremendous pain most of my life. I was born into conflict, drama, and problems I never asked for. When I was young, I didn't know what was going on. I was a child. However, as I grew older, I had to begin to deal with reality.

Throughout the years, God has had to rewrite in my mind and my heart some of the ideas planted in me at a young age. One way He did that is by showing me the Scriptures. The poverty mindset was one of the biggest curses I faced growing up. Every day I have to remind myself that God delights in prospering me (Psalm 35:27). I have also had to learn how to rule my spirit (Proverbs 25:28) and guard my tongue (Proverbs 21:23). Sometimes I have to remind myself that if I don't say it, people can't repeat it. Having seen so much arguing and fighting for most of my life, I've witnessed the devastation of an unruled spirit and an unbridled tongue.

If I did not have an active prayer life, I would have never found myself - I would have never come close to realizing who I was in Christ. When I write, speak, or minister, I never say I am perfect. I am far from it! What I will say is I am not afraid to publicly talk about the Bible or Jesus Christ. I am not ashamed to talk about God. Some people assume this means I am somehow spiritually superior. My answer? Nope. I just love God, and I love His Word. That is a generational blessing I received on both sides of my family line.

Putting His Word into practice has been a lifelong journey. The carnal flesh nature is always looking for a way to wiggle its way out. Your prayer life is personal. It is multi-dimensional, and even at times, seemingly a little irreverent when you are alone with God. God is your Father. You tell Him everything. He already knows. He knows when you're happy, when you're sad, and when you're angry. I cannot tell you how many times I've been in my car alone screaming because I am so frustrated, and guess what? God never left me. He didn't stop talking to me.

God draws near. Coward and God do not go together. When things are tough, God is a warrior. He fights for His children. This is why the prophet Zephaniah says, "The LORD your God is among you; He is mighty to save. He will rejoice over you with gladness; He will quiet you with His love; He will rejoice over you with singing." (Zephaniah 3:17 BSB) God has a supernatural way of calming us down and assuaging our fears. Bringing peace during the midst of difficulty and pain is God's specialty. Walking with God is not a neat, packaged deal. It gets messy. You have an adversary, and when you walk with God the enemy is going to stir himself up (and others) to come against you.

Jesus warns us in John 15:18-20 (BSB), "If the world hates you, understand that it hated Me first. If you were of the world, it would love you as its own. Instead, the world hates you, because you are not of the world, but I have chosen you out of the world. Remember the word that I spoke to you: 'No servant is greater than his master.' If they persecuted Me, they will persecute you as well; if they kept My word, they will keep yours as well." Your prayer life can be a war zone. It is where battles are fought.

The devil would love to wipe out your family line. More than once I have seen and heard in the Spirit the devil asking God to let him take my life. If he can wipe me off the face of the earth, he can keep me from testifying about the Lord. Of course, God has not allowed that. If the devil had it his way, he would wipe out all believers. The good news is God is in full control. The Lord may allow certain things in our lives we don't want, but He sets boundaries the enemy cannot cross. The Book of Job is a great book of the Bible to read on this topic.

Praying is how we build a hedge of protection from the wiles of the enemy. Praying for others is the catalyst for seeing hearts and minds change. My great-grandfather, grandfather, and father all had similar struggles growing up. They were all hard workers, talented, and intelligent. However, they all have had to deal with the exact same thinking: they felt like they weren't good enough and even had to deal with some self-hatred.

As the firstborn son of the firstborn son of the firstborn son of the firstborn son, guess what I have had to deal with for years? The exact same thing. I inherited my fathers' work ethic, talent, and smarts, but I also inherited the struggle of frustration, not feeling good enough, and self-hatred. All of them loved the Lord, and they loved the Word of God. Fortunately, I inherited that as well. The way I have had to combat the generational curse of "not being good enough" is by lots and lots of prayer and Scriptures. This generational curse was a big one. It has put limitations on all four of us.

The good news is I believe that curse is shattered in Jesus' name. I believe no matter what was handed to me as I came out of the womb is going to stop me from fulfilling my destiny. The same is true for you. You are brand new in Jesus Christ (2 Corinthians 5:17). Another way the enemy will try to stop you from your destiny is by working overtime to convince you to stay down once you've fallen. You drink too much alcohol, you look at something you shouldn't have, you cross some boundaries, you give in to the addiction, or you cave to whatever the struggle is.

If the enemy can convince you that your struggle is something you can never overcome or bounce back from he's got you. It's the snare of the fowler that God wants to deliver you from (Psalm 91:3). The devil can't keep you down when you run to the Father. Psalm 124:7-8 (NIV) says, "We have escaped like a bird from the fowler's snare; the snare has been broken, and we have escaped. Our help is in the name of the LORD, the Maker of heaven and earth." Jesus is the trap breaker. He destroys the hunter's evil schemes set against you.

As you actively pray, you are stirring your strength up in the Lord. Proverbs 24:16 tells us that though we were to fall seven times, we get up again. We bounce back. We overcome. Your prayers are like the wings of an eagle. As you pray, your spiritual wings are causing you to lift off and rise above. Spiritual doors open and close when you pray. Your prayers are heard. They matter. They are powerful and carry divine authority. As Christ's Spirit gives you the words, your prayers create an unshakeable establishment.

Revelation 3:7-8 (NKJV) tells us, "These things says He who is holy, He who is true, 'He who has the key of David, He who opens and no one shuts, and shuts and no one opens': 'I know your works. See, I have set before you an open door, and no one can shut it; for you have a little strength, have kept My word, and have not denied My name.'" There is an open door set before you. Though you may have little strength, you are still standing by faith.

The name of the Lord is your strength. He is who you call on in times of need. He is available to you at any given moment in time. He is continually speaking, if you will look, listen, and believe. Right now God is turning things around. He is causing things to work together for the good. He is breathing new life into your spirit. His zeal is stirring up a great work in you. Your spiritual eyes have vision to see what couldn't be seen before. The light is on. Now it's time to pray.

SCRIPTURE READING

Zephaniah 3:15-17

Psalm 91:1-7

Matthew 6:5-8

Revelation 3:7-13

QUESTIONS TO ANSWER

When is the best time of day you can set aside, undistracted, to be alone with God and pray?

Where has the enemy tried to snare you and convince you that you are trapped? This could be an addiction, a bad habit, or some type of wrong thinking. What is a Bible verse you can memorize to remind you of the truth that you are free?

When you mess up or give in to temptation, what are different ways you can get back up and stir up your spirit to keep going? What moves you to want to live for the Lord all the more? This could be stopping to pray, turning on Christian music, reading the Bible, talking to a faith-filled friend or loved one, or attending a service.

Chapter Thirteen

4:44

God is always speaking. He speaks through His Word, through prophets, through other people, through songs, through visions and dreams, through creation, through colors, sights, and sounds, and through numbers. There is nothing physical or spiritual that exists apart from Jesus Christ. If this is true, then that means God can speak through anything physical or spiritual. Colossians 1:15-17 (NASB95) says, "He is the image of the invisible God, the firstborn of all creation. For by Him all things were created, both in the heavens and on earth, visible and invisible, whether thrones or dominions or rulers or authorities— all things have been created through Him and for Him. And He is before all things, and in Him all things hold together."

God speaks through numbers. Having minored in mathematics and computer science in college, I am always amazed at how perfectly numbers work together. Studying algebraic equations and learning through Calculus 3 how all things numbers work, I always knew there was a God who was the creator of numbers. As a matter of fact, there is an entire book of the Bible called Numbers. It's the fourth book of the Bible. Numbers are important to God. He is the inventor of mathematics.

In the Hebrew alphabet, there are 22 letters. Each letter has a numeric value. Gematria is the method of adding up the numerical sum of each letter in a word or phrase in Hebrew.

Words in Hebrew are given a gematria value by adding up the numbers of each letter in the word. For example, the name Jesus has a numerical value of 444 in English Gematria. The letters of Jesus with their numerical value: J(60), E(30), S(114), U(126), S(114). Add the numbers 60 + 30 + 114 + 126 + 114, and you get 444.

From a very young age, I have always been fascinated by numbers. Numbers jump out at me on road signs, grocery receipts, time clocks, and more. When I was young I may not have realized it, but God was often speaking through the numbers I was seeing. When I was older, I learned more about the Hebrew alphabet, which is alphanumeric. The fourth letter of the Hebrew alphabet is dalet. Dalet means "door", "pathway", or "creation". We see several fours in God's creation: the four winds, the four elements (earth, water, air, and fire), the four seasons (fall, winter, spring, and summer), the four regions (north, south, east, and west), and the four lunar cycles (new moon, first quarter, full moon, and last quarter).

Not long ago, I kept seeing the number "444" everywhere. Driving down the road, I'd see 444 on the mileage. I would look at the clock, and it was "4:44". It kept happening over and over. As I looked into what the number four meant in Hebrew, I realized God was telling me to create. Be creative. Use His creation as an artist and a writer to make something new. Whenever I sit down to write, I am creating pages of a book or newsletter that have never existed before. When I add new lines and movie scenes to my screenplay, I am bringing something new into creation.

Brothers and sisters, we are creators. God has designed His children to be innovative and intelligent. We received this talent from Him. Today we have more products, technological developments, and information available to us than any other time period in history. In these last days, God is speeding things up as knowledge continues to increase (Daniel 12:4). If God had a time clock for this period we are in, it would say, "4:44". It's time to create. Get busy, Church. There are books to write, movies to produce, businesses to launch, children to raise, people to reach, needs to be met, and callings to be fulfilled. Everyone in God's family has a role and a divine purpose for the era we are living in.

Dalet, which is four, also means "door". When we see dalet, we are seeing the word "door". Next time you see "444", in Hebrew you are seeing "door-door-door". God has opened doors for you to walk through. Likewise, He has shut other doors to protect you. When Jesus says, "I am the door," (John 10:9) He is saying, "I am the dalet." The dalet of God is Jesus Christ. He is the only dalet that gives us access to God's presence and the Kingdom of Heaven. We go in and out of Heaven in the spiritual realm through Jesus. When we learn how to go into Heaven, retrieve what we need, and bring it to Earth, we are fulfilling our call to bring Heaven to Earth (Matthew 6:10).

In Heaven is a massive library full of stories and testimonies chronicling the lives of God's children. These books have already been written before time began. This means that before you were born, God already knew you. He already knew when you would be born and who you would become. Psalm 139:16 (NLT) tells us, "You saw me before I was born. Every day of my life was recorded in Your book. Every moment was laid out before a single day had passed." This means you have access through the dalet, that is Jesus Christ, to see some of what is recorded in God's library. Reading God's books about your life or others is called prophecy.

The only way to prophesy is by the Spirit of the Lord. Jesus is the perfect example of prophecy being fulfilled. From the beginning of creation, God spoke concerning the coming Messiah. The Old Testament is full of messianic promises. How did these prophets know what the Messiah, Jesus, was like before Jesus was ever born? The way they knew was that they were hearing and reading from God's library of books in Heaven. Everything has already been written. God was enabling His prophets to speak what He already knew.

In the same way, there are pages and pages and pages - too many to count - regarding your life.

Psalm 139:17-18 (NLT) says, "How precious are Your thoughts about me, O God. They cannot be numbered! I can't even count them; they outnumber the grains of sand! And when I wake up, You are still with me!" The things God has written and planned for your life are so many that they can't even be numbered. There are great works prepared for you to accomplish that are from Heaven (Ephesians 2:10). One way Jesus knew who He was and what He was going to do when He arrived on earth is He knew the Scriptures. He knew the Law and the Prophets. He knew what was said concerning Himself.

In the same way, just as prophecy was sent to God's people before Jesus was born for the Messiah to fulfill, so God has sent His prophetic words ahead of you. You are alive today because God predetermined for you to be here. The Lord spoke, and your time to be born was set. You are designed with a calling and a purpose from above. When I kept seeing 4:44 on the clock (and have several times since starting to write this chapter), it was God reminding me that He is right on time. It was a sign sent to make me wonder. Hebrews 2:4 (NLT) tells us, "And God confirmed the message by giving signs and wonders and various miracles and gifts of the Holy Spirit whenever He chose."

Does God still speak through signs and wonders today? Absolutely. Are there false signs and wonders? Yep. (See 2 Thessalonians 2:9) How can we tell the difference? By being grounded in God's Word and knowing His Spirit. When I see different numbers on the clock or the odometer, I know it is God reminding me of His promises. It is just one more way God is speaking to me. Every time I see 4:44 I think of my calling. I think of the movie script I am writing. I think of the books I am working on. I think of my friends who are so creative and talented.

When I see 4:44, I feel in my spirit God saying, "It's time to create!" Like the angels who stirred the water in John 5:4, it's like God's angels are stirring things up to create something new. This is how books are written. This is how business ideas are formed. This is how some of the biggest evangelists and church planters in the world started. The waters were stirred by angels. The world you live in is a result of some big waters being stirred. The generations before us had the courage to start families, launch a business, move to a new place, and build a life not knowing what might happen next.

Many of the ceilings and limitations our ancestors once faced have been removed. We have medicines, vehicles, airplanes, computers, electronic devices, advanced farming techniques, and more that make life better. While we sometimes take these modern developments for granted, somebody once paid the price in order to make the world a better place. The same is true in our faith. The gospel has advanced all over the world because people sacrificed their lives to share Jesus. While the message of salvation is free, the great commission Jesus gave (Matthew 28:18-20) to his disciples cost them their lives.

The sacrifice of others has made a pathway we so freely enjoy. The Bible is now more easily accessible than ever before. Teachings abound on any Scripture you read. We are living in the Information Age. Your calling is unique to the current era we are in. God hand-picked you to be His vessel for this time period. If you feel a little different from the rest of the crowd, that just means God has set you aside for something special. The Apostle Paul tells us to not go along with those who are not following the Lord.

He says in 2 Corinthians 6:14-18 (NCV), "You are not the same as those who do not believe. So do not join yourselves to them. Good and bad do not belong together. Light and darkness cannot share together. How can Christ and Belial, the devil, have any agreement? What can a believer have together with a nonbeliever? The temple of God cannot have any agreement with idols, and we are the temple of the living God. As God said: 'I will live with them and walk with them. And I will be their God, and they will be My people. Leave those people, and be separate, says the Lord. Touch nothing that is unclean, and I will accept you. I will be your father, and you will be My sons and daughters, says the Lord Almighty.'"

Walking away from darkness is the first step to discovering who you are meant to be. The devil will gladly receive anyone willing to advance his satanic agendas. There are many creative people in the world who are not walking with God. If you refuse to use your talents for God, Satan will use them instead. There is no in-between. There are only two masters and two kingdoms: the Kingdom of God and the Kingdom of Darkness. The only reason Satan has any power is because God has allowed it. He has given mankind free will to choose whom they will serve.

When the devil offers you the world, there is always a catch. Money, fame, popularity, pleasure, and self-indulgence are his game. It's how some of the most gifted ministers in the world are led astray. Give a man some money, and you will see what's really in his heart. You cannot serve both God and mammon (Matthew 6:24). How do we overcome these deceptions that anyone can succumb to if caught off guard? Faith. Your faith in Jesus is the most valuable asset you have in defeating the enemy.

The Apostle John says in 1 John 5:4-5 (NLT), "For every child of God defeats this evil world, and we achieve this victory through our faith. And who can win this battle against the world? Only those who believe that Jesus is the Son of God." We are living in a world full of people who are defined by the Bible as spiritual wolves and swine. They will destroy you spiritually if you are not wise. This is why Jesus tells us, "Look, I am sending you out as sheep among wolves. So be as shrewd as snakes and harmless as doves." (Matthew 10:16 NLT)

We must become wise if we are going to rise above the course of this world. The good father in the Book of Proverbs says this: "Get wisdom, get understanding; do not forget my words or turn away from them. Do not forsake wisdom, and she will protect you; love her, and she will watch over you. The beginning of wisdom is this: Get wisdom. Though it cost all you have, get understanding. Cherish her, and she will exalt you; embrace her, and she will honor you. She will give you a garland to grace your head and present you with a glorious crown. Listen, my son, accept what I say, and the years of your life will be many." (Proverbs 4:5-10 NIV)

Recently I walked into work, and I could sense in the air a lot of tension and warfare going on. Before I entered the door that morning, I heard the Spirit tell me, "You are exactly where you are supposed to be." Little did I know, the Lord was encouraging me, because He already knew what a grueling day it was going to be. As the day went on, it was extraordinarily stressful. (Ever been there?) As I walked, I could see a white snake following me in the Spirit. However, it wasn't demonic. It was actually from the Lord; to my right side, I saw a dove. They followed me everywhere I walked.

I felt in my spirit to guard my words very carefully, to be wise as a serpent and gentle as a dove. As the day went on, all sorts of issues began to come up. I began to have to fight off my own emotions and troubled thoughts. The grief process decided to visit work that day too. That week I was grieving the death of my mom from a few months ago. By the end of the day, I was physically and emotionally drained. The day ended when I finally got home, and one of my dogs had "marked" the shop vac by my roommate's door. I had to clean the mess, and finally, I could retire.

Friends, not every day is going to be a cakewalk. The next day was much better. Many issues had been resolved, or at least I had more peace about them. The ensuing week I covered a lot of ground in my screenplay writing. One morning before writing I saw in the Spirit two men wrestling. I sensed one was defending me, and one was trying to attack me. I knew it was the Lord showing me an angel and a dark force were at war with one another, and He was allowing me to see it. The enemy was trying to stop me from writing. He was trying to demolish what I was creating. It didn't work.

In the same way, the enemy is going to take his best shot to keep you from fulfilling your destiny. He is going to fight to try and keep you from doing something new for God. The devil hates it when it's 4:44 time. He doesn't want God's people to create, innovate, and thrive. His desire is to beat down the church and silence the prophets. He is always twisting and using words of faith to try and destroy us. The good news is God is our defender. Our focus is on Him and what He can do.

Today God is calling you to pursue wisdom and understanding. He is calling you to the dalet, to the open door. Behind this door is life and freedom. Here there is a deeper trust and understanding of the ways of God. This door is Jesus Christ, the Son of God. Apart from this door, we cannot enter the Kingdom of Heaven. There is no other door by which we can be saved. For generations, men and women have entered through the dalet and found new life. People have been set free of illnesses, addictions, and curses. Entire nations have been born in response to this door of eternal life.

Jesus has made a pathway for you to walk on. All of your steps are ordered by Him (Psalm 37:23). You play a marvelous role in the history of God's creation. He marked you on His timeline to carry out a task that only you can accomplish. Before He said, "Let there be light," He knew your name and your calling. He is your God. You belong to Him. He purchased you with the precious blood of His Son (1 Corinthians 6:20). God wants to glorify His name in and through you. Right now, in the spirit of creativity, the clock says, "4:44". It's time to create.

It's time to step out in faith and do what has never been done before. God has equipped and empowered you to fulfill your God-given destiny. Whatever your talents are - whether hidden and buried or already fully known - they are being activated by the Spirit of Christ dwelling in you. Your zeal for the Lord is growing stronger. Your desire to create something new is growing by the day. The dalet is open. New experiences and ideas are flooding your mind and heart.

You are going to new levels of victory and success like never before. The hand of God's favor is heavy upon you. The oil of Aaron is anointing your life with ease, peace, and promotion (Psalm 133:2). Every wicked way is being destroyed. The Lord is making your crooked places straight (Isaiah 45:2). He is making the straight and narrow clearer than ever before. You are walking into your Promised Land.

SCRIPTURE READING

Daniel 12:1-4

Proverbs 4:1-10

John 10:1-9

Colossians 1:13-20

QUESTIONS TO ANSWER

Do you believe God speaks through His creation? Through numbers, colors, sights, and sounds?

How does God speak to you? What do you feel like He is saying to you right now?

What is something new you believe God is calling you to do, but you haven't stepped out in faith and tried yet? What are some new experiences you would like to have, and you need to ask God to help make them possible?

Chapter Fourteen
HAVING A WEALTHY MIND

Your mind is powerful. What you think will dictate the direction and quality of your life. If your thought life is poor, your life is going to be poor. Developing and training your mind to think the way Christ thinks is the call of every believer. If we are to be like Him, we must learn to think like Him (1 Corinthians 11:1). When Jesus walked on the earth and it was His time to publicly display His ministry in front of the world, He never worried about a lack of resources or the inability to heal. Why? Jesus had a wealthy mind.

Jesus knew where He was from. He was from Heaven. Not only was He from Heaven, but He had access to all of Heaven's resources. He was not limited by the natural world and the laws of nature. When the disciples could only find five loaves of bread and two fish to feed the 5,000 men plus women and children, Jesus was not concerned. What did Jesus know that no one else did? Jesus had what the people lacked. Jesus had faith. Faith means Jesus knew the end result from the beginning.

Jesus knew what He was going to do. He knew what God the Father was going to do, so multiplying food was no big deal for Him - rather, it was a big deal to the disciples. Seeing the miraculous was normal for Jesus. He was from Heaven. Jesus' goal in feeding the 5,000 wasn't just to fill empty stomachs; it was to teach His followers a lesson. John 6:5-6 (NLT) says, "Jesus soon saw a huge crowd of people coming to look for him. Turning to Philip,

He asked, 'Where can we buy bread to feed all these people?' He was testing Philip, for He already knew what He was going to do."

Jesus is the fulness of faith. He is Creator God in human form. He is the example and the way. While in human form, Jesus knew what He was capable of. In the same way, you need to know what you are capable of. There is a gift Jesus gave us after He physically left the earth and took His seat at the right hand of the Father (Mark 16:19). Jesus gave us Himself. He gave us His Spirit. Not only did He give us His Spirit, but He gave us access to His mind and to His way of thinking. The Apostle Paul understood this incredible gift. It's how he was able to write almost half of the New Testament.

In his letter to Corinth, the Apostle Paul writes, "No one can know a person's thoughts except that person's own spirit, and no one can know God's thoughts except God's own Spirit. And we have received God's Spirit (not the world's spirit), so we can know the wonderful things God has freely given us. When we tell you these things, we do not use words that come from human wisdom. Instead, we speak words given to us by the Spirit, using the Spirit's words to explain spiritual truths.

But people who aren't spiritual can't receive these truths from God's Spirit. It all sounds foolish to them and they can't understand it, for only those who are spiritual can understand what the Spirit means. Those who are spiritual can evaluate all things, but they themselves cannot be evaluated by others. For, 'Who can know the LORD's thoughts? Who knows enough to teach Him?' But we understand these things, for we have the mind of Christ." (1 Corinthians 2:11-16 NLT)

You have been given the mind of Christ. Whatever Christ did, so can you. Signs, wonders, and miracles weren't just a Bible thing or an ancient apostle thing. It's a Christian thing. All Christians have the same power living in them that Jesus had. It's the exact same Spirit, and there is only one Spirit (Ephesians 4:4). Jesus knew in Heaven where He was from that there was no sickness. There was no lack of resources. There was no lack of creativity or life. There was no death. It's Heaven!

He also knew the power of Heaven flowed through Him, and because of His death on the Cross and His resurrection He knew you and I would have that exact same power of Heaven flowing through us. This is why Jesus said it was better that He left the earth because He knew if He just stuck around that the Spirit would not come and revolutionize the earth (John 16:7). Jesus knew there would be millions and millions of people like Himself. They would know God, and they would have His power to do the work He desired to accomplish in the world.

What hinders the flow of the Spirit is unbelief and sin. A wealthy mind can be bogged down with anxiety and fear through unbelief and sin. Sin is like a chain. It's a snare that drags us down. Hebrews 12:1 (NIV) says, "Let us throw off everything that hinders and the sin that so easily entangles." Falling into sin or unbelief is like falling into quicksand. It can get you stuck and in a bind really fast. Our flesh nature is impoverished. The brain run by the flesh nature is addicted to sin. It cannot and will not stop. God knew none of us could overcome the flesh without His help. That's why He sent His Son to set us free from this enslavement.

When you transform your mind by thinking in line with the Spirit, your mind is no longer governed by the flesh nature. The Apostle Paul tells us in Romans 8:5-9 (NIV), "Those who live according to the flesh have their minds set on what the flesh desires; but those who live in accordance with the Spirit have their minds set on what the Spirit desires. The mind governed by the flesh is death, but the mind governed by the Spirit is life and peace. The mind governed by the flesh is hostile to God; it does not submit to God's law, nor can it do so. Those who are in the realm of the flesh cannot please God. You, however, are not in the realm of the flesh but are in the realm of the Spirit, if indeed the Spirit of God lives in you. And if anyone does not have the Spirit of Christ, they do not belong to Christ."

Jesus had the fulness of God's Spirit living in Him. He could send a disciple to get money out of a fish's mouth to pay an unjust tax (Matthew 17:24-27). He could turn water into expensive, aged wine at a wedding (John 2:1-11). He multiplied groceries more than once for the masses. He saved the sick from countless medical bills (Mark 5:25-26). Jesus was fully aware of the cost of things in this world. Just like today, it could be expensive to live in those days. Not once was Jesus worried about how He was going to meet a need or pay for it. He already knew how. His mind was not focused on the world.

Likewise, we should not worry. The root of the worry weed grows in the famished soil of fear. The root of the good seed grows in the rich soil of faith. Where we plant our minds and hearts is important. We must stay in faith if we want to rise above fear and grow. You are created for good works. You have the power to create wealth. Moses tells us in Deuteronomy 8:18 (BSB), "But remember that it is the LORD your God who gives you the power to gain wealth, in order to confirm His covenant that He swore to your fathers even to this day."

When I entered this world as a baby, I was born into a family that had made tremendous wealth, then lost most all of it. The dynamics I went through as a child - how I was taught to think about money - were vast. On the one hand, I was the grandson of a banker. On the other hand, I was also the child of family dysfunction and financial ruin. The conflict in my mind about money and wealth only escalated as I grew older. By the time I got to college, I was determined to be very successful financially. However, at the time I didn't realize all the mental and emotional conflict within me had to play itself out throughout my twenties. By the end of my twenties, I was carless, moneyless, and virtually homeless. I was bankrupt.

I constantly battled Satan's lie that I was poor at handling money, that I could never get out of poverty, and that I was accursed financially because of where I came from. These deep-rooted thoughts were a generational curse. I was repeating some of the same negative, unbiblical thoughts that ran through the family line. In one side of my mind I knew I was anointed by God to prosper. On the other side, I saw the current financial state I was living in. What the promises of God said and what the reality of my life was were contradictory.

It took most of my thirties to break out of the poverty mindset. I had to work extremely hard, but I began to see God create a brand new life in me. I was no longer broke all the time as I worked and declared God's promises each day. I spent the money I made as wisely as I knew how. I developed a wealthy mind by constantly going to war with the poverty mindset I inherited. Before long, I began to see far-out prophetic words from the past having to do with Wall Street and cars and books (and more) be fulfilled before my very eyes.

Today I am further along than I ever thought possible. It took years, even decades, to break a ruthless, merciless financial generational curse. When I think of having a wealthy mind, I think of all I had to go through to destroy a poverty mind. What we think on a daily basis will dictate the direction of our lives in the long run. Proverbs 23:7 (NASB) says, "For as he thinks within himself, so he is." When God gets ready to do something big in your life, He may spend years reprogramming your thinking in order to prepare you.

We live in a microwave-speed society. We want everything quick - the sooner the better. The problem with the microwave mindset is that it usually compromises the quality. God does not microwave His promises for your life. He spends as long as He needs in order for you to be ready for what He's called you to do. I knew for many years that I would be handling large sums of money and stewarding resources one day. I studied business in college. I was around "business talk" all the time growing up. The problem was there were a lot of things I learned growing up that God had to retrain me in. There were generational curses I needed deliverance from.

The good news is God has grown me into where I am today. I still have a long way to go, but I am definitely headed in the right direction. The same is true for you. Whatever stage of life you are in, God will meet you where you are. He can take generational curses, unfair situations, and heartache and turn it all around (Romans 8:28). God is your season finale. He is your deliverer. He will see you through to the other side of the battle. Psalm 35:27 (NASB95) tells us, "Let them shout for joy and rejoice, who favor my vindication; And let them say continually, 'The LORD be magnified, Who delights in the prosperity of His servant.'"

God loves seeing you prosper. The adversary will work overtime trying to convince you otherwise. This is why we need to continually play the Word of God in our hearts and minds. It's how we build faith. It's how we silence the devil's accusatory voice. When God speaks a promise to you, what you usually see when you receive that word looks totally opposite. When God spoke to Abraham and Sarah about having a son, the opposite looked true. Abraham and Sarah were old. Sarah had a zero percent success rate at getting pregnant in the past. Based on the facts and history, there was no way Abraham and Sarah were having a baby.

If you had told me when I was twenty-nine that I would write four books and be completely out of debt in less than eight years, I would have looked at you like you were crazy. My life was ground zero. It would have seemed impossible. Maybe there is a part of your life that looks like ground zero. You may feel like Sarah, 89 years old and barren. You have one thing to hold on to that Sarah had. Sarah had God's promise. She had the word of the Lord. God's word always overrides what history and "facts" may suggest.

At the ripe old age of 90, Sarah had a son. She named him Isaac, which means "he laughs". His name is about laughing because Sarah laughed when she overheard God's messengers tell Abraham that she would have a baby by the next year (Genesis 18:12). When Sarah's son grew up, he was blessed greatly. Genesis 26:12-13 (NASB95) says, "Now Isaac sowed in that land and reaped in the same year a hundredfold. And the Lord blessed him, and the man became rich, and continued to grow richer until he became very wealthy."

God's promises always result in life, abundance, and overflow. When Jesus was obedient to the point of death on the Cross, He created a global overflow of God's salvation and praise in His name after His resurrection. The prophet Isaiah declares in Isaiah 61:11 (ESV), "For as the earth brings forth its sprouts, and as a garden causes what is sown in it to sprout up, so the Lord GOD will cause righteousness and praise to sprout up before all the nations." Jesus sacrificing Himself saved the whole earth. Now anyone from any nation can come to know God personally in Jesus' name.

You have a wealthy mind already because you have the mind of Jesus Christ, the Son of God. When you tap into the wealth that is already in you, ideas and mental resources are unlimited. If you are looking for God's power and great resources, look no further. It's already inside of you. Luke 17:20-21 (NJKV) tells us, "Now when He [Jesus] was asked by the Pharisees when the kingdom of God would come, He answered them and said, 'The kingdom of God does not come with observation; nor will they say, 'See here!' or 'See there!' For indeed, the kingdom of God is within you.'"

God's everlasting Kingdom dwells on the inside of you. His Kingdom is the living water that never runs dry (John 7:38). God has given you the ability to turn on the pump to your soul. He has made your spirit to flow like a river. Endless songs, stories, and revelations continually flow from this river. The Apostle Paul says in Ephesians 5:18-20 (NIV), "Do not get drunk on wine, which leads to debauchery. Instead, be filled with the Spirit, speaking to one another with psalms, hymns, and songs from the Spirit. Sing and make music from your heart to the Lord, always giving thanks to God the Father for everything, in the name of our Lord Jesus Christ."

Being grateful for what God has already given us is how we stir up more of God's favor and blessing. Every time Jesus performed a miracle, He gave glory to His Father in Heaven. His purpose was to honor the Father and to do what the Father told Him. Likewise, we should always look up and give thanks. We are here to serve the Lord and do what pleases Him. When we pray before a meal with our children and grandchildren, we are showing the next generation how important it is to give thanks to God for His provision.

When we take time to pray with our spouses, parents, and children, we are building a family legacy of faith for generations to come. God can take any barren situation and bring new life. The Lord says in Isaiah 41:17-18 (NLT), "When the poor and needy search for water and there is none, and their tongues are parched from thirst, then I, the LORD, will answer them. I, the God of Israel, will never abandon them. I will open up rivers for them on the high plateaus. I will give them fountains of water in the valleys. I will fill the desert with pools of water. Rivers fed by springs will flow across the parched ground."

The Lord is filling the dry desert places of your soul with springs of water. You are being refreshed and renewed from the inside out. There is no lack or want in the presence of the Lord. His power and resources are unlimited. His ability to multiply and create is infinite. The good news is that same power lives in you. That power is the Holy Spirit, whom God has given to all who believe in Him. The only thing stopping this power from flowing is you. When you release your faith, having a made-up mind to believe all things are possible, God will do far beyond what we can ask, think, or imagine (Ephesians 3:20).

You have been given a powerful mind, capable of creating so much life and victory. As you learn to take authority over the battlefield of thoughts each day, capturing each thought for Christ (2 Corinthians 10:5), you are going to see the Lord work in marvelous ways. The retraining of your mind starts by feeding yourself the Scriptures. It begins by praying and talking to God as your friend. He is your counselor, comforter, and confidant. Tap into the wealthy mind you have been given. Because of Christ's Spirit, Heaven lives in you. Let the river of His life flow freely in and through you.

SCRIPTURE READING

Genesis 26:12-17

Deuteronomy 8:16-20

Matthew 17:24-27

1 Corinthians 2:11-16

QUESTIONS TO ANSWER

What are some things taught to you growing up that do not align with the mind of Christ and the Scriptures?

What does having a "wealthy mind" mean to you? Where can you see opportunities instead of limitations that are already in your life with this wealthy mind God has given you?

Is there any unbelief in your heart that you need to repent of and ask God to help you with? *(If so, go ahead and tell Him!)*

Chapter Fifteen
THINKING IN COLOR

God sees in color. His throne is full of color, and He is colorful by nature. Just as God speaks through words, sounds, and numbers, so He speaks through His colorful Creation. The Apostle John describes God's throne room in the Book of Revelation, saying, "Immediately I was in the Spirit; and behold, a throne was standing in heaven, and someone was sitting on the throne. And He who was sitting was like a jasper stone and a sardius in appearance; and there was a rainbow around the throne, like an emerald in appearance." (Revelation 4:2-3 NASB)

Sardius is a red precious stone. It is the same stone found in the priest's chestpiece. Various colorful stones are used to represent the tribes of Israel. Moses instructs the priests in Exodus 28:15-16 (NLT), "Then, with great skill and care, make a chestpiece to be worn for seeking a decision from God. Make it to match the ephod, using finely woven linen embroidered with gold and with blue, purple, and scarlet thread. Make the chestpiece of a single piece of cloth folded to form a pouch nine inches square."

When God instructs Moses on what to tell the people, He is very precise in His instructions. He gives Moses the exact color and size for everything he is to make. The Lord is attentive to every detail, as Moses is commanded to make a replica of what is in Heaven. Hebrews 8:5 (BSB) tells us, "The place where they serve is a copy and shadow of what is in heaven. This is why Moses was warned when he was about to build the tabernacle: 'See to it that you make everything according to the pattern shown you on the mountain.'"

The Israelites and the priests had to be exact in replicating all that Moses told them. They were creating a copy of what Heaven was like. When Jesus ascended into Heaven, He sat down in the eternal sanctuary, not the manmade one. Hebrews 8:1-2 (NLT) says, "Here is the main point: We have a High Priest who sat down in the place of honor beside the throne of the majestic God in heaven. There He ministers in the heavenly Tabernacle, the true place of worship that was built by the Lord and not by human hands."

Heaven is truly a very colorful, bright place. If the Torah (Law of Moses) is only a shadow of Heaven, then Heaven must be all the more magnificent. The colors and stones found in the priests' breastplate alone are stunning. Exodus 28:17-20 (NKJV) tells us, "And you shall put settings of stones in it, four rows of stones: The first row shall be a sardius, a topaz, and an emerald; this shall be the first row; the second row shall be a turquoise, a sapphire, and a diamond; the third row, a jacinth, an agate, and an amethyst; and the fourth row, a beryl, an onyx, and a jasper. They shall be set in gold settings."

Each colorful stone is a representation of something important to the Lord. Exodus 28:21 (NLT) says, "Each stone will represent one of the twelve sons of Israel, and the name of that tribe will be engraved on it like a seal." God's heart for His people is shown in each stone. The Lord loves the twelve tribes of Israel, and He chose twelve precious stones to express it. The same God who chose colorful stones to represent His heart is the same God who is seated with a rainbow around His throne.

Before Satan used modern culture to try and pervert the meaning of the rainbow, God had already established the rainbow as His covenant for all generations to come to never flood the earth again (see Genesis 9:12-17). Furthermore, God's resting place is full of color. When the Apostle John saw God's chair, he saw a rainbow around it. He saw the full spectrum of colors. The reason John saw the full spectrum of colors is because God is Light (1 John 1:5).

When light shines through a prism like glass - and before the throne is like a sea of glass - then the light bends and separates into red, orange, yellow, green, blue, indigo, and violet. This process is called dispersion. When God's light bursts forth from Himself, it causes marvelous colors to reflect His glory as it touches everything it encounters. Precious stones fill the throne room of God. He is awesome and worthy of everlasting praise. When we get to Heaven, we are going to be amazed by the colorful sights and sounds. What we see now is only a shadow of what we are going to see in eternity.

Thinking in color is how God thinks. This comes naturally to artists and entertainers. It's how God wired them. They tend to think differently from the rest of us because many people tend to think in black and white. While truth is black and white, it is also full of color. When people read the Bible, they are reading black and white (plus red letters for Jesus' words, of course!). However, God wants us to see past black and white. He wants us to think and see in full color.

Our spiritual vision can be compared to the evolution of the television. The first electronic TV was demonstrated on September 7, 1927, by Philo Taylor Farnsworth in San Francisco. Black and white televisions became available to the public in 1936. While the color TV was first available in 1954, it took thirty years for color television to become more common. In 1984, stereo sound broadcasting allowed for a more immersive audio experience. The first 3D TV was introduced in 2010. Furthermore, high definition began to replace standard definition in the early 2000s.

What we visualize in our minds about God and His Word is much like watching TV. When we think about God and meditate on His Scriptures, our minds show us something on the mental TV screen. We can physically see what is on a TV screen, but what we see playing on the screen of our minds is even more important. The mind is where faith plays out. It's where the flesh and the Spirit are at war with one another (Galatians 5:17). We are all subject to internal conflict because we are all born with a fleshly, carnal nature. In Christ, we can overcome this internal conflict, but we never escape the physical body until it's time for us to leave this world.

When people get bored with God and religion, it's because they are watching an old-school, outdated TV in their minds. There is no color. The sound is only mono. There's no remote control (which was invented in 1950). Quite frankly, what they are thinking about God and religion seems irrelevant to real life. This is where the devil wants God's people. The enemy does not want you to see and know God in full color, sight, and sound. Instead, he wants you bored with your faith. Keep it black and white and out of sight.

Friends, there is nothing boring about God. He is full of life. The arts and entertainment belong to the Lord. God designed entertainment to be something to enjoy. He knows we need time to relax and take a break from responsibilities and the daily grind. When life gets too serious, it might be time to take a deep breath and put on a comedy. Let yourself laugh. Even in the Scriptures, people entertained. Some people entertained in a good way; others not so much. Hebrews 13:2 (BSB) tells us, "Do not neglect to show hospitality to strangers, for by so doing some people have entertained angels without knowing it."

Hospitality, comfort, entertainment - all of these things were created by God to be a blessing. One of the most hospitable characters in the Scriptures is Joseph. Joseph was likely an entertainer by nature and had a colorful imagination. His father made him a coat full of different colors. The colorful coat symbolized Joseph's favor with his father Jacob

(Genesis 37:3). Despite betrayal by his own brothers, Joseph continually floated to the top wherever he went.

First, he was thrown into a pit before becoming sold into slavery. He rose to the top in his master Potiphar's house, ultimately managing all the Egyptian official owned (Genesis 39:4). When Potiphar's wife tried to seduce Joseph, he fled and was falsely accused. He was then thrown into prison, where he continued to prosper. There, he gained favor and took charge over the entire jail under the chief jailer's charge (Genesis 39:22-23). Several years later, Joseph interprets a dream and stands before Pharaoh. It is before Pharaoh that God exalts Joseph to the most powerful man on earth next to Pharaoh himself (Genesis 41:40-44).

The coat of many colors was a foreshadowing of the favor and promotion on Joseph. Joseph was destined for great success, and it was marked by a colorful tunic. Jacob was thinking in color when he handed his son Joseph a new garment. Later on, when the priests were given instructions for placing the different colors of stones on the priestly breastplate, the tribe of Joseph was given a black onyx stone. The color black is the only color not in the color spectrum.

When light shines on the primarily black stone, it absorbs all wavelengths and colors of visible light. All other colors are reflections of light, except black. Black is the only color that can exist in nature without any light at all. Joseph's dark stone shows the hope and faith Joseph had when all the world was against him. Against all odds, Joseph continually overcame. Even in a murky pit or blacked-out prison cell, Joseph still had faith to rise up and overcome. It is no coincidence that Joseph's stone is represented by the dark onyx stone.

God did for Joseph what He wants to do for all who trust in Him. The psalmist declares in Psalm 40:2 (NLT), "He lifted me out of the pit of despair, out of the mud and the mire. He set my feet on solid ground and steadied me as I walked along." When we are in a dark season or difficult trial, God sees everything that is happening. He knows what is happening, even in the dark. Psalm 139:11-12 (NLT) tells us, "I could ask the darkness to hide me and the light around me to become night— but even in darkness I cannot hide from You. To You the night shines as bright as day. Darkness and light are the same to You."

Nothing can hide from God's light. Jesus tells us in Mark 4:21-23 (NLT), "Then Jesus asked them, 'Would anyone light a lamp and then put it under a basket or under a bed? Of course not! A lamp is placed on a stand, where its light will shine. For everything that is hidden will eventually be brought into the open, and every secret will be brought to light. Anyone with ears to hear should listen and understand.'" The truth is seen in full color. The intentions and motivation of every person are transparent before the Lord. This is why listening to the Holy Spirit is so important. God knows things we sometimes don't.

Hebrews 4:12-13 (NIV) says, "For the word of God is alive and active. Sharper than any double-edged sword, it penetrates even to dividing soul and spirit, joints and marrow; it judges the thoughts and attitudes of the heart. Nothing in all creation is hidden from God's sight. Everything is uncovered and laid bare before the eyes of Him to whom we must give account." I cannot tell you how many times there are opportunities that come across my path, and the Spirit tells me, "No, don't do that." People can make us offers that seem too good to be true, or we can use conventional wisdom to try and make good choices, but the Lord already knows where any given path may lead.

Recently, I was offered to try and represent a certain product for a company. I had been praying about doing more of this type of work in the marketplace, so it seemed like an answer to my prayers. However, I thought about the offer, and I then heard the Lord say,

"No. I have something better in store for you. Something much bigger." Everything about the offer seemed harmless, like there was nothing to lose. Without God's counsel, I would have likely gone ahead with the offer. It would have consumed some more of my time (which I have very little extra these days), and it may have been a dead end.

The Scriptures tell us in Proverbs 19:21 (NASB95), "Many plans are in a man's heart, but the counsel of the LORD will stand." One of the aspects of the believer's journey is learning to walk close to God and listen closely to His voice. The Lord has already seen the path, and He knows what lies ahead. Psalm 37:23 (NLT) says, "The LORD directs the steps of the godly. He delights in every detail of their lives." Throughout life, I have learned God is in the minute details as much as He is in the big plan. He cares about your future, and He pays attention to the desires of your heart.

Years ago, I went with a ministry team in Los Angeles to Hollywood Boulevard at night. It was one of the best street ministry experiences I've ever had. Many prayers were made, and the Holy Spirit moved mightily right in the center of Hollywood. Several words from the Lord were given. In our praying, I remember having a vision of blue shoes. I saw myself working, and I distinctly remember wearing these blue shoes. Fast forward a few years, and I began working for my family back home. I bought a new pair of shoes and guess what color they were? Blue. For over ten years, I have worn blue shoes to work in.

When I saw blue shoes in the Spirit, I had no idea I would work in blue shoes for over ten years. At the time, I wasn't wearing blue shoes. The color of the shoes was not as big of a deal as the work God had called me to do, but it is a detail that God wanted to highlight. In the Bible, blue is represented by the Hebrew word "tekhelet". Tekhelet is mentioned 49 times in the Scriptures and was used in the High Priest's clothing, the tabernacle, and priestly tassels. Blue signifies heaven and God's divine presence. Blue is the color beneath God's feet.

Exodus 24:10 (NLT) tells us, "There they saw the God of Israel. Under His feet there seemed to be a surface of brilliant blue lapis lazuli, as clear as the sky itself." Again, the prophet Ezekiel says, "As they stood with wings lowered, a voice spoke from beyond the crystal surface above them. Above this surface was something that looked like a throne made of blue lapis lazuli. And on this throne high above was a figure whose appearance resembled a man." (Ezekiel 1:25-26 NLT) As I began to see the different ways God speaks to His people, colors began to take on a whole new meaning.

Every time I see blue now, it tells me God is speaking. When I had this revelation about the color blue several months ago, I continually saw the color blue. Blue cars, blue shirts, blue cans - everywhere I turned, blue jumped out at me. The Holy Spirit was showing me that God is always speaking. Romans 1:20 (NLT) says, "For ever since the world was created, people have seen the earth and sky. Through everything God made, they can clearly see His invisible qualities—His eternal power and divine nature. So they have no excuse for not knowing God."

Throughout history, civilizations have worshipped in all sorts of ways. Of course, only the God of Israel is the one true God, but people knew there was something more divine behind all that they could see in the natural world. From generation to generation, God has always made Himself known. When one generation passes, God must reveal Himself to the next generation. Because of God's faithfulness, He has made sure to make His glory known throughout the ages. All of creation testifies that God exists and that He is good.

Museums around the world are full of artwork, sculptures, and ancient artifacts that remain from both Christian and pagan worship. Since the beginning of time, mankind has had eternity set in the human heart (Ecclesiastes 3:11). Sometimes, it seems people live like they are invincible. That could be in part because before the fall of Adam, we actually were invincible. We were made to live forever. However, sin put a death sentence on the human body, so God had to send His Son to redeem us.

One day, we will be like Him. We will no longer be subject to a body that is destined to die. We will be given immortality, the greatest gift of all. This eternal gift is available to all generations, and it is by putting one's faith in Jesus Christ that we are saved from death. All who believe in Jesus will one day stand before God's glorious, colorful throne. The sights, sounds, and colors will be far beyond even the most beautiful, rare, and exotic places on Earth. God's invitation to join Him for eternity is available to everyone, to all who receive Him as their personal Lord and Savior.

SCRIPTURE READING

Exodus 28:15-20

Ezekiel 1:26-28

Romans 1:20-23

Revelation 4:1-3

QUESTIONS TO ANSWER

What's your favorite color? *(Mine is blue.)*

Has God ever spoken to you personally through His creation *(i.e., sights, sounds, colors)*? If so, how?

How can you let your light shine like Jesus says in Mark 4:21? What gifts has God given you that can be used to glorify Him?

Part Four

DEVOTE

"Your hearts therefore shall be wholly devoted to the LORD our God, to walk in His statutes and to keep His commandments, as at this day."
1 Kings 8:61

Chapter Sixteen
HAVING A HISTORY WITH GOD

Throughout my life, there have been distinct, unforgettable encounters I've had with the Lord that have impacted the course of my life. These encounters leave a mark. I can remember experiences years, even decades, later - and in great detail. When I was a teenager, I remember the night I felt the presence of an angel telling me I was going to move. It was a controversial decision for a 15-year-old, but it was the right one. When I was 18, I remember the evening I decided to withdraw my application to a prestigious Ivy League university with great conviction. Another controversial decision was made, with God confirming I made the right choice. My high school counselor, Mrs. Casey, told me it may be time for me to "widen my nets" for finding the right university.

Shortly afterward, I found the college of my dreams. It was like university euphoria for over a year. God selected the perfect campus in the world for me to learn, grow, and prosper. At age 25, the Spirit of God brought me to the floor at a revival gathering in Kansas City on New Year's Eve. I was going to Hollywood. A few weeks later, another life-altering move was made, and I was living in Los Angeles. At 29, the Spirit of God came over me strongly. I was to write a book. A few months later, God created an author. "Tasting the Goodness of God" was published. I haven't stopped writing since. At age 40, the Lord told me I was set free. Big decisions were made - also controversial - but I knew I made the right ones. My 40th birthday also happened to be the last day I ever spoke with my mom before she died.

These are just a few of the many different defining moments in my life. These moments are what have given me a powerful history with God. The longer I live, I remember the different times God performed a miracle or revealed a major life-changing decision to be made. The longer we walk with God, the deeper our faith naturally becomes. We weather storms with God. We go through the ups and downs of life. As time goes on, our spiritual maturity develops. It becomes more and more difficult for the enemy to pull us away from the Lord because our roots have grown much deeper than when we first began.

Your history with God is one of your biggest weapons against the enemy. When the enemy tries to tell you you're not going to make it, that you are sinking, you can recall all of the times God delivered you. He did it for you before, and He's going to do it for you again. Proverbs 3:5-6 (BSB) instructs us, "Trust in the LORD with all your heart, and lean not on your own understanding; in all your ways acknowledge Him, and He will make your paths straight." The key for anyone trying to straighten out their life is to trust in the Lord with their heart. When a person finally surrenders their heart to God, He causes the pieces to start coming together.

Conventional wisdom and good choices can help people have a better life, but only fully surrendering to the Lord is going to give a person real meaning and leave an eternal impact. Salvation goes beyond a one-time conversion experience. Walking with God is a lifelong journey. We don't just "accept Christ" at the altar, and that's it. Unfortunately, that tends to be the mindset in Western culture. You receive Jesus for salvation, then go on living as you please. You have fire insurance, and you're good to go - almost like you were buying car insurance in case of a wreck. Only call God when you're in a bind. He's the 9-1-1 God of your life, but not the Lord of it.

Throughout the Scriptures, we see men and women who walked with God for most, if not all, of their lives. They certainly were not perfect, but they had a personal relationship with their Creator. They were fully devoted to Him. The same thing should be true for every believer today. There isn't one area of your world God should (or could) be excluded from. "In all your ways" acknowledge Him means we consider the Lord in every single decision we make. Compromise is where the devil can gain a foothold to bring unwanted destruction.

I have learned that it is usually difficult to do what is right. It takes discipline. It's like exercising. It can be uncomfortable. Following God usually requires a level of sacrifice. However, like exercising, there are benefits for doing what God tells us to do. When we live for Him from the heart, it releases His saving power to go to work. The psalmist declares in Psalm 103:1-5 (ESV), "Bless the LORD, O my soul, and all that is within me, bless His holy name! Bless the LORD, O my soul, and forget not all His benefits, Who forgives all your iniquity, Who heals all your diseases, Who redeems your life from the pit, Who crowns you with steadfast love and mercy, Who satisfies you with good so that your youth is renewed like the eagle's."

Throughout my life, I have had to deal with trauma - trauma in my childhood, trauma in my teenage years, and trauma at various points in my adult life. After experiencing trauma, I have noticed God always fills my life with sweet things. He has never abandoned me after I've gone through serious pain. He has never kicked me when I was down. Others have, but not God. He doesn't operate that way. He is good. He is good at all times. It is in the pit and in the setback that a history of God's faithfulness develops and becomes extraordinarily personal. Knowing Him is what carries us through.

God wants to show you Himself in such a way that when things go south, you remember the past times He showed up and expressed His lovingkindness. The Lord is your deliverer. You are guaranteed to have troubles in this life, but God promises to deliver you through every trial (Psalm 34:19). The Lord is devoted to His children. Whenever we go through heartache or loss, He draws near in a special way (Psalm 34:18). His divine presence has a way of giving us supernatural peace when there is no explanation.

Proverbs 16:20-21 (NASB) tells us, "One who pays attention to the word will find good, and blessed is one who trusts in the LORD. The wise in heart will be called understanding, and sweetness of speech increases persuasiveness." There is a sweetness about God's Spirit. When He ministers to us, His love is like honey to the soul. He heals us. He reminds us that He is always good. When I was in college, I went through a dark season of questioning many things, including my salvation. I had been greatly harmed by a legalistic ministry.

I had to take a semester off from college because I literally could not think or function from the control of being under such a rigid, harmful mindset. During that brief time away from college, God spoke to me in a special way. It was like God gave me cotton candy to sweeten my soul and nurture me back to life. He showed me His love, His laughter, and His life. When I finished my break, I went back to college. I not only finished, but I prospered greatly. The darkness and the pain were buried. Since that season of darkness, I have never questioned my salvation again. To wonder whether God loves you or not, whether you are saved or not, going back and forth, is a horrible place for any believer to dwell.

Sanctification is a lifelong journey. Where you start with God is not where you end with Him. It's like being in a marriage. It's a covenant. The only difference is that marriage doesn't last into eternity (there is no marriage in Heaven; see Matthew 22:30). The milestones and failures of my faith are many. There have been bright seasons of breakthrough and victory, and there have been dark seasons of failure and loss. The one thing God asks in return through all of it is that we stay devoted to Him.

Just as a husband and wife are called to support one another "in sickness and in health", so we are in partnership with the Lord. Whenever we are drifting away from the Lord or have drifted away, I always tell people now is the time to return to Him. He is ready to receive you at all times. Jesus tells us, "All that the Father gives Me will come to Me, and the one who comes to Me I will certainly not cast out." (John 6:37 NASB95) Friends, God is merciful. Truly, He is far more merciful than any of us. How many of us can say our lives have been spared because of God's divine protection?

Back in 2012, a superstorm arose in the Atlantic Ocean. At the time, I was staying in New York City. As the storm began to approach, I had already booked my trip home, but it was still several days away after the superstorm was to make landfall. However, at the last minute, the airlines decided to allow anyone to change flights free of charge to avoid the massive hurricane. The night before the storm hit, I was able to book a flight. As my airplane was taking off the next day, Hurricane Sandy was just about to hit. I remember thanking God for delivering me from the storm as I watched on the news the tiny island of Manhattan being pummeled. Roadways and subways were flooded, and there were massive power outages all over the city. $19 billion in damages were inflicted on New York City alone by Sandy.

I have never forgotten how God safely brought me out of harm's way. That memory has always served as a reminder that God is my personal deliverer. When I read Scriptures and psalms of how God delivered David or the Israelites, it becomes more personal. It's not just a Bible verse to stand on. It's a Scripture I've experienced firsthand because I've lived through life events when I needed the Lord's divine protection. Having a personal history with God makes your relationship with God just that: Personal. While it is good to be around other believers, attend services, sing praise songs, and read the Bible, at the end of the day, God desires a close relationship with each and every one of His children.

Church attendance is not what gets a person into Heaven. What gets a person into Heaven is their faith in Jesus Christ and in knowing Him. There will be people on judgment day who went to a church somewhere their whole life, and tragically, they never knew Him. It was just religion, something they do on Sunday morning. This is why Jesus warns us in Matthew 7:21-23 (NLT), saying, "Not everyone who calls out to Me, 'Lord! Lord!' will enter the Kingdom of Heaven. Only those who actually do the will of My Father in heaven will enter. On judgment day many will say to Me, 'Lord! Lord! We prophesied in Your name and cast out demons in Your name and performed many miracles in Your name.' But I will reply, 'I never knew you. Get away from Me, you who break God's laws.'"

I say this not to invoke fear in you but to make a strong point. Jesus is a person, and we need to know Him for ourselves. There is a mindset in the culture today that says you can just "get saved" and then go do whatever you want. Sin away. You're under grace. God's my judge, not you. It's all good… It doesn't work that way. We have to make Jesus our personal Lord. The word "lord" means someone who has authority, power, and rule over you. They are the one in charge. We are living in the Last Days. This means the level of deception is only going to increase. The ones who truly know the Lord will overcome. However, there have been and there will continue to be many who fall away.

Great ministers, preachers, and churches will rise and fall. Worship bands will create Godly music, then some will turn away from the faith years later. The longer I live, the more I see even the one-time spiritually "great" fail to stay steadfast. This is why the Word always encourages us to stay devoted to the Lord in this dark hour. The Apostle Paul teaches us that undistracted devotion is a blessing. While he is writing the church, he tells us it is better not to marry (as did Jesus; see Matthew 19:10-12). He says in 1 Corinthians 7:35 (NASB95), "This I say for your own benefit; not to put a restraint upon you, but to promote what is appropriate and to secure undistracted devotion to the Lord."

When we are single, it is much easier to remain undistracted in serving the Lord and keeping our eyes on the things above. The Apostle Paul explains in 1 Corinthians 7:32-34 (NLT), "I want you to be free from the concerns of this life. An unmarried man can spend his time doing the Lord's work and thinking how to please Him. But a married man has to think about his earthly responsibilities and how to please his wife. His interests are divided. In the same way, a woman who is no longer married or has never been married can be devoted to the Lord and holy in body and in spirit. But a married woman has to think about her earthly responsibilities and how to please her husband."

As someone who has been single virtually almost all of my life, I can attest to this statement as being true from experience. Not having a wife or children has allowed me to be extraordinarily focused and disciplined in my work. I am fully aware that most people could not do what I do for a living. They have family responsibilities - taking care of a wife and supporting their children. Because of my childhood - namely, financial struggles and instability in the home - I chose not to marry at a younger age. The desire for stability, independence, and having a deep faith drives me to work as hard as I do.

The Lord revealed to me at the ripe young age of eight my need for Jesus Christ in order to go to Heaven. I have known Jesus as my Lord and Savior my whole life. My personal history with God through Christ is longer than many. Some people don't come to truly know Christ until they are a teenager or in adulthood. Learning God's Word and experiencing His presence in childhood developed a foundation of faith that has carried me through a turbulent life. My history with God has shaped and molded me into who I am today. I wouldn't trade my faith for anything in this world - riches, fame, or even health. Nothing is more valuable than your faith in Jesus.

Generational faith is a blessing. People who were fortunate enough to grow up in a Christian home may not realize how blessed they truly are. Proverbs 22:6 (BSB) tells us, "Train up a child in the way he should go, and when he is old he will not depart from it." To this day, there are principles and values that guide my life and decision making that I learned at a very young age - Bible verses, sermons, and songs from as young as I can remember that influence the way I think, feel, and believe. What we learn in childhood plays a huge role in who we become when we are older.

This is why it is so important to take your kids to church. Encourage your kids to grow in their faith. Protect your kids from things that may spiritually harm them. Tell them why something is right or wrong. Use the Scriptures. Jesus was protective of children, and so should we. Jesus says in Luke 17:2 (BSB), "It would be better for him to have a millstone hung around his neck and to be thrown into the sea than to cause one of these little ones to stumble." Children have more faith than anyone in the world. When a person crushes that faith or misleads a child, it is a serious offense in God's eyes.

In order to see revival and see new generations of strong believers, we must reach the children and the youth. When people come to know Christ at a younger age, they develop a history with God that runs deep. Over 80% of Christians accept Christ as children and early youth. The odds of a person accepting Christ decline with age. Some have referred to the "4-14 Window" as the age group that is most likely to accept Christ as their personal Lord and Savior. While God can save any person at any age, the statistics certainly make a point about the importance of our youth and younger children.

God loves revealing Himself to people when they call out to Him. Right now, I believe God's hand is stretched from Heaven towards you. He is calling you to a deeper relationship with Him. He is doing a new thing. The words of Isaiah the prophet are calling out to you, "Behold, I am about to do something new; even now it is coming. Do you not see it? Indeed, I will make a way in the wilderness and streams in the desert." (Isaiah 43:19 BSB) God is stirring up that childhood faith that lives in the heart of every believer.

He is reminding you of the times, the moments, when He was there for you. He is the God of the valleys and the mountains in your life. In the days of feast or famine, God has been and always will be your Provider. He is renewing your hope, causing you to rise above obstacles and opposition, and catapulting you to the next level of your destiny in Jesus' name.

SCRIPTURE READING

Proverbs 22:4-6

Isaiah 43:16-21

Matthew 18:1-7

1 Corinthians 7:32-35

QUESTIONS TO ANSWER

What is the youngest age you can remember that you had a personal encounter with God?

When was a time that God delivered you from harm? Have you thanked Him for protecting you?

What does being devoted to the Lord look like for you personally? *(For example: going to church, reading your Bible every morning, playing worship music, etc.)*

Chapter Seventeen
GOD REVEALED THROUGHOUT TIME

Since the beginning of time, God has made Himself known to whom He so chooses. In the beginning, He walked in the Garden of Eden with Adam and Eve (Genesis 3:8). After the fall, God intentionally hid Himself. He allowed mankind to decide whether or not they were going to do what is right. Eve's first two sons, Cain and Abel, demonstrated freewill. Abel chose to do what was right, while Cain turned out to be a murderer (1 John 3:12). Abel was the blessed one, murdered by his own brother, Cain. Cain was called evil and accursed (Genesis 4:11). The Lord restored the Messianic lineage when Eve gave birth to her third son, Seth (Genesis 4:25).

This shouldn't be hard to believe, but mankind has been a hot mess since the very beginning. Adam and Eve ate from the wrong tree. Their firstborn son murdered their other son, and the saga of a messed-up mankind world continues to this very day. It's a tough pill to swallow, but the very first person to be born from the womb turned out to be a murderer. Despite all of man's shortcomings, God never separated Himself from us completely. His ears are always open, even when people are behaving wrong. Genesis 4:26 (NIV) says, "Seth also had a son, and he named him Enosh. At that time people began to call on the name of the LORD."

The Lord answers those who call on Him. When people called on the Lord in the

Scriptures, God would answer. The same is true today. When people call on the Lord from a sincere heart, He listens and responds. We should always make prayer our first priority when we wake up every day. King David says in Psalm 5:3 (NIV), "In the morning, LORD, You hear my voice; in the morning I lay my requests before You and wait expectantly." Those who have faith, trusting in God's power and not their own, are the ones God uses in a special way to demonstrate His glory.

God continually revealed Himself to various prophets and people of faith in order to influence politics and global change as recorded in the Bible. Shadrach, Meshach, and Abednego would not kneel before the golden statue of Babylon's King Nebuchadnezzar, and their supernatural deliverance from a blazing furnace led to a global decree that all nations were to honor the God of Israel (Daniel 3:29). When Hagar was kicked out of Abraham's house, God revealed Himself as the Deliverer for her son Ishmael who was sure to die from lack of water. Ishmael was to one day become a great nation because of God's blessing (Genesis 21:14-20).

In the Book of Judges, God raised up twelve different judges (leaders) to bring deliverance to His people. God used Othniel, Ehud, Shamgar, Deborah, Gideon, Tola, Jair, Jephthah, Ibzan, Elon, Abdon, and Samson to defeat Israel's oppressors. After Joshua's death, the Israelites continued to turn away from the LORD, and God continued to bring deliverance. While God did allow His people to suffer for not following Him, He never abandoned them.

The ultimate deliverer God sent was His one and only Son, Jesus. Jesus put an end to the power of sin. He set God's people free. Romans 8:1-4 (NKJV) says, "There is therefore now no condemnation to those who are in Christ Jesus, who do not walk according to the flesh, but according to the Spirit. For the law of the Spirit of life in Christ Jesus has made me free from the law of sin and death. For what the law could not do in that it was weak through the flesh, God did by sending His own Son in the likeness of sinful flesh, on account of sin: He condemned sin in the flesh, that the righteous requirement of the law might be fulfilled in us who do not walk according to the flesh but according to the Spirit."

When the Lord sent the Holy Spirit to dwell in the heart of the believer, He established a new covenant built upon grace. The tedious Law given by Moses in the Old Testament had no power to make a person righteous. The Law of Moses was a tutor pointing us to faith in Jesus Christ, who was to come some 1,400 years later. The Law only proved to show just how sinful we really are! Adam sinned in the Garden of Eden, and the curse of sin spread to all of us.

Romans 5:19-21 (NLT) tells us, "Because one person disobeyed God, many became sinners. But because one other person obeyed God, many will be made righteous. God's law was given so that all people could see how sinful they were. But as people sinned more and more, God's wonderful grace became more abundant. So just as sin ruled over all people and brought them to death, now God's wonderful grace rules instead, giving us right standing with God and resulting in eternal life through Jesus Christ our Lord."

When Jesus was revealed to be the Anointed One sent by God from Heaven as His Beloved Son, it literally changed everything, even the dating system on our calendars. We went from B.C. (Before Christ) to A.D. ("Anno Domini", Latin for "in the year of our Lord"). The course of human history changed dramatically because Jesus marked the end of one era - the ancient times - to the beginning of another - the Last Days. We have been living in the Last Days since the gospel of Christ's salvation was preached. God the Father has chosen to reconcile the world through His Son Jesus.

John 14:21-24 (NLT) says, "'Those who accept My commandments and obey them are the ones who love Me. And because they love Me, My Father will love them. And I will love them and reveal Myself to each of them.' Judas (not Judas Iscariot, but the other disciple with that name) said to Him, 'Lord, why are You going to reveal Yourself only to us and not to the world at large?' Jesus replied, 'All who love Me will do what I say. My Father will love them, and We will come and make Our home with each of them. Anyone who doesn't love Me will not obey Me. And remember, My words are not My own. What I am telling you is from the Father who sent Me.'"

Jesus' response to Judas is interesting. God doesn't always reveal Himself to anyone and everyone all of the time. Judas thinks Jesus needs to tell the whole wide world who He is. Jesus explains to Judas that not everyone loves Him, that only those who honor what He says truly love Him. Furthermore, Jesus shares with the disciples that He didn't make His teachings up. God the Father in Heaven is the One who told Him all that He was sharing with His followers.

You would not share your son or daughter with the whole world, especially when they are younger. As a good parent, you try to shield and protect your child from the world as best you can. The world has evil in it. God did not reveal His Son, His one and only Son, to the whole world all at once. When the people did finally figure it out, they killed Him. From the outside looking in, that's disturbing. As believers, we know why Jesus had to be crucified, but it just shows how sinful mankind really is apart from truly knowing God.

Another teaching Jesus taught is not to share things of great spiritual value with just anyone. It can backfire really quickly. He tells His disciples in Matthew 7:6 (NASB), "Do not give what is holy to dogs, and do not throw your pearls before pigs, or they will trample them under their feet, and turn and tear you to pieces." Dogs and pigs are animals of figurative language here. People who are dogs don't appreciate your advice or spiritual counsel. Pigs don't want what you have to offer, because they are incapable of seeing its value, are spiritually ignorant, and are hostile.

Likewise, God knows when to reveal Himself to anyone's heart. He knows how to speak to all people. This does not mean that everyone is going to receive Him, but there is no one on this planet whom God does not know everything about. It's what makes Him God. The Lord has raised up and torn down kings, kingdoms, and civilizations since the beginning of time (Daniel 2:21). When a person asks me if a person goes to hell because they never heard the gospel, I have to consider the all-knowing power of God. There isn't going to be someone in hell who isn't supposed to be there, and there isn't going to be someone in Heaven who isn't supposed to be there. We may be ignorant and lack knowledge, but God certainly is not.

The Holy Spirit has been at work since long before any of us were born. Whether or not God's people obey does not determine what God has already ordained. The Lord already knows all who are His, and those who are not (2 Timothy 2:19). However, God does bestow great responsibility on His people to carry out His work. In every generation, in every civilization, and in every era of time, God has been in full control over His creation.

In the days of Noah, the world had gone far astray. Genesis 6:5-8 (BSB) tells us, "Then the LORD saw that the wickedness of man was great upon the earth, and that every inclination of the thoughts of his heart was altogether evil all the time. And the LORD regretted that He had made man on the earth, and He was grieved in His heart. So the LORD said, 'I will blot out man, whom I have created, from the face of the earth—every man and beast and crawling creature and bird of the air—for I am grieved that I have made them.' Noah, however, found favor in the eyes of the LORD."

Noah stood out to the Lord because of his devotion. The next verse goes on to say, "Noah was a righteous man, blameless in his generation; Noah walked with God." (Genesis 6:9 BSB) Only Noah, his wife, his three sons, and their wives were saved in the global flood. Can you imagine a world that is so corrupt that only eight people are spared and considered worthy to be saved by God? The level of wickedness must have been so extreme that our minds could not (nor would not want to) fathom it.

God revealed His plans to Noah because He knew Noah loved Him. The same is still true today. God knows you love Him. If you didn't, you probably wouldn't be reading this book! God is the Word (John 1:1). When we read His Word and fall more in love with His Word, we are really falling more in love with Him. I believe Noah talked back and forth with God like you would talk back and forth with your spouse or very best friend.

Furthermore, Noah needed God's divine protection living in such a violent world (Genesis 6:13). Your science teacher will likely never tell you this, but the dinosaurs were on the earth before the flood. Ever seen Jurassic Park? Not very friendly reptiles. When the flood broke forth, those massive dinosaurs (including the violent ones) were wiped out, and now we have what's called fossil fuel under the earth. The Earth is not billions of years old. It's how old the Bible says it is.

The devil has craftily used false prophets in these last days to deceive the masses. Consider all of the false teachings that stem from Charles Darwin's misleading "findings" at the Galapagos Islands. Satan has had a heyday deceiving the world with Darwinism. I've never been a fan of Charles Darwin. Even at a young age, I knew the guy was full of it - way too many false conclusions and erroneous assumptions for much of it to be even remotely true. A giraffe's head would explode millions of times by bending to drink water before it could "evolve" into a modern-day giraffe. Makes no sense to me (because it's a lie). God made giraffes (perfectly) on the sixth day, and Adam named them in the Garden of Eden. Fortunately, some scientists are finally catching up to what God said happened in His Word.

In the times we are living in now, it is going to become more and more like the days of

Noah. The deception will increase, as will the violence. Jesus already warned us that these days are coming. He tells us in Matthew 24:37-39 (NKJV), "But as the days of Noah were, so also will the coming of the Son of Man be. For as in the days before the flood, they were eating and drinking, marrying and giving in marriage, until the day that Noah entered the ark, and did not know until the flood came and took them all away, so also will the coming of the Son of Man be."

Jesus is coming back. This final revelation will be greater than anything we have ever seen. When people teach on the rapture, which is the supernatural transport of believers from earth to Heaven at Christ's Second Coming, they usually point to Jesus' next statements. In the next two verses, Jesus says, "Two men will be working together in the field; one will be taken, the other left. Two women will be grinding flour at the mill; one will be taken, the other left." (Mathew 24:40-41 NLT)

Just as the Lord snatched up Noah, his wife, and his children in an evil day, so the Lord is going to snatch up those who follow Him in these Last Days. We do not know exactly when, but we know by what is going on in the world now that the day is getting even closer (Matthew 24:36). We are called by the Lord to be prepared and to live as though He could come at any given time (Matthew 24:42). The good news is if you are already walking with God, talking to Him, and seeking to please Him, His return will be exciting and rewarding. Communion and fellowship with God were the plan from the beginning.

The Lord longs for and loves His people. He delights in revealing more and more mysteries of His glorious kingdom to all who want to know Him (Luke 12:31-32). God can turn any mystery into a victory when we turn the situation we are dealing with over to Him. God is a personal and intimate God. He can and does custom build any solution to any problem you are ever going to have. The Lord specializes in performing the impossible. When we keep God first, He does the heavy lifting.

From generation to generation, the Lord visits and revisits those who are seeking Him. 2 Chronicles 16:9 (NIV) tells us, "For the eyes of the LORD range throughout the earth to strengthen those whose hearts are fully committed to Him." When you surrender your heart to God, His eyes are going to see it. Angels are drawn to people who are seeking God with their whole heart. Throughout history, there have been times of war and times of peace. Men and women who lived through the world wars of the early 20th century saw unimaginable horrors of death and destruction while fighting to save the world from evil regimes. The Holocaust of God's people, the Jews, has left the world with a permanent memory of anti-Semitism at its worst.

Right now, you are called to stand strong for what is right in this generation. Just as the freedom fighters before us resisted Adolf Hitler and the Nazi regime, exposed the concentration camps, and set captives free, so we are called to stand against evil today. Biblical principles and Christianity are under attack like never before. The hatred of the Jews is rising to levels not seen since Nazism. We are living in an era when it is not popular to stand on the Word of God. When you resist evil and stand, God is going to show Himself strong.

There are political groups and Christian organizations God has called you to partner with to bring about positive change. You are not alone in your fight for good in this world. The Apostle James reminds us in James 4:17 (NLT), "Remember, it is sin to know what you ought to do and then not do it." With over 150,000 Christian non-profit organizations in the United States alone, there is a place for every believer to help advance God's Kingdom. For some, God may be calling you to start your own specific ministry.

From day to day, God is revealing knowledge and truth (Psalm 19:2). For millennia, God has been speaking. Right now, I believe God is speaking directly to you. He is speaking to your heart. There are seeds of greatness planted into the fabric of your soul. As you turn your mind and the intentions of your heart towards the Lord, He is causing dreams and desires that are from Him to come alive. He is building a life of fulfillment that comes from within. His Spirit is stirring in you like the stirring of many waters.

As you walk with the Lord, you are leaving a legacy of faith for the generations to come. You are creating a testimony because of the inner workings of the Holy Spirit. As you stand on God's Word, you are going to see victory and fulfillment because His Word never returns empty or unfruitful (Isaiah 55:11). The reward for having a heart fully devoted to Jesus is immeasurably awesome and beyond anything our earthly minds can fully grasp. Seek Him first every day and expect His goodness to overtake every area of your life.

SCRIPTURE READING

Genesis 21:14-20

2 Chronicles 16:7-9

Romans 5:17-21

James 4:13-17

QUESTIONS TO ANSWER

When was a time God revealed Himself to you personally in a very special way?

Do you ask God to show Himself and speak to you directly? What are ways you can experience more of God's presence? *(For example: listening to worship music, reading the Bible, talking to a Spirit-filled friend, attending a church service, praying with a friend or your spouse, etc.)*

Is there a Christian organization or political group supporting Judeo-Christian values you feel led to be more involved with in order to bring about positive change in the world?

Chapter Eighteen
PSALM 78

One of the most powerful prayers in the Scriptures that focuses on sharing who God is with future generations is found in the Book of Psalms. A Levite by the name of Asaph, appointed by King David to lead worship at the Temple, wrote Psalm 78. This historical psalm marches through the past marvelous acts of God and Israel's times of rebellion. Psalm 78 is a great prayer and a wonderful reminder to recall the acts of God in our lives and to repent when we mess up or go through a period of rebellion. Furthermore, Psalm 78 is an order from the Lord to share the good news of His Kingdom and His faithfulness with future generations.

Asaph begins with a call to attention, saying, "O my people, listen to my instructions. Open your ears to what I am saying, for I will speak to you in a parable. I will teach you hidden lessons from our past— stories we have heard and known, stories our ancestors handed down to us. We will not hide these truths from our children; we will tell the next generation about the glorious deeds of the Lord, about His power and His mighty wonders." (Psalm 78:1-4 NLT) Instilling Biblical truths into children at a young age is a gift that lasts for generations.

When we are taking our children and grandchildren to church, encouraging our youth to attend church camps, and share our faith when we are able, we are planting deep-rooted seeds that last far longer than the amount of time it took to plant the seed. The payoff for sowing God's Word into our children's hearts is far greater than the sacrifice it takes to get them to church and learning the Word. When I was in high school, my younger brother (who is over nine years younger than me) would be shuttled to the Awana Club every Wednesday evening by my great-grandmother. Each week at Awanas, my curious little brother would memorize Scriptures.

My brother was sharp, even at a very young age. He could learn and retain the Awana verses easily. Years later, he still knows the Word very well. He knows the Word, perhaps more than others, because my great-grandmother chose to get up and take him to Awana Club each week when he was young. If she couldn't take him, she made sure he got there. Proverbs 22:6 (BSB) tells us, "Train up a child in the way he should go, and when he is old he will not depart from it." Those seeds planted in his heart many years ago are still there today.

The psalmist goes on to say in Psalm 78:5-7 (NLT), "For He issued His laws to Jacob; He gave His instructions to Israel. He commanded our ancestors to teach them to their children, so the next generation might know them — even the children not yet born — and they in turn will teach their own children. So each generation should set its hope anew on God, not forgetting His glorious miracles and obeying His commands." When we spend time and energy reaching our youth and our children, we are establishing a generational blessing that can repeat itself.

If alcoholism, drug abuse, and immorality run rampant in your family line, you can put a stop to the generational curse by instilling different values in your children. In place of a curse, you can establish a blessing. It's God's will to set free entire family generational lines from the clutches of the enemy. The devil doesn't just want to destroy individuals. He wants to wipe out entire family lines. When we or the ones we love act out in rebellion towards God, we operate in sin. In time, sin invokes curses and destruction that can last for generations (Exodus 20:5).

This is what happened to Israel's ancestors when they were in the wilderness. Psalm 78:8 says Israel's ancestors were stubborn, unfaithful, and rebellious. They refused to give their hearts to God even though He performed great miracles, like parting the Red Sea to escape Pharaoh's army (Exodus 14:21-22), giving them water from a rock in the dry wilderness (Exodus 17:6), and leading them by cloud during the day and fire by night (Psalm 78:13-16). The Lord performed miracle after miracle, and yet Israel's ancestors refused to listen or obey.

The same is true today. There are people who have tasted the goodness of God continually, and they still refuse to give their hearts to Him. This is what happened when Jesus tells the story of the rich man and Lazarus, who was a beggar covered in sores. When they both died, Lazarus was carried by angels to Heaven. The rich man was thrown into hell. The rich man never repented of his deeds and refused to honor God's Word. Lazarus knew nothing but a lifetime of great sorrow and suffering.

Luke 16:25-31 (NIV) says, "But Abraham replied, 'Son, remember that in your lifetime you received your good things, while Lazarus received bad things, but now he is comforted here and you are in agony. And besides all this, between us and you a great chasm has been set in place, so that those who want to go from here to you cannot, nor can anyone cross over from there to us.' He answered, 'Then I beg you, father, send Lazarus to my family, for I have five brothers. Let him warn them, so that they will not also come to this place of torment.' Abraham replied, 'They have Moses and the Prophets; let them listen to them.' 'No, father Abraham,' he said, 'but if someone from the dead goes to them, they will repent.' He said to him, 'If they do not listen to Moses and the Prophets, they will not be convinced even if someone rises from the dead.'"

When Abraham tells the rich man that his five brothers have Moses and the Prophets, he was basically saying, "Your brothers have the Bible. Let them read it." Before Christ, there were the Law and the Prophets given to God's people. Today, we have the Law and the Prophets (Old Testament) and the New Testament. Nearly everyone on the planet has access to a Bible. Abraham was making a point when he told the rich man in hell that his brothers wouldn't listen, even if someone rose from the dead. Jesus did rise from the dead, and today there are still many who do not believe in God's Word.

Israel's rebellion in the wilderness is a warning to the world today. If God punished the Israelites after He performed so many signs, wonders, and miracles, then He will certainly punish those who will not acknowledge or honor Him still. The good news is that God is patient, merciful, and kind. However, every single person in the world gets the choice of whether or not they will receive Him and receive His Word into their heart. People making mistakes is not what displeases the Lord. What displeases Him is refusing to believe or trust Him. Psalm 78:21-22 (NLT) tells us, "When the LORD heard them, He was furious. The fire of His wrath burned against Jacob. Yes, His anger rose against Israel, for they did not believe God or trust Him to care for them."

Whenever we find ourselves in a place of disbelief, it's a good time to look up and repent before the Lord. When we find ourselves fretting about money or a child, it's time to look up and remember who our Caretaker is. Our Caretaker is in Heaven. He sees and knows all things. If the Israelites had genuinely turned their hearts towards the Lord in the wilderness, they would have left a much different legacy than what we read about today in the Scriptures. Instead, God had to start over with a brand new generation in order to fulfill Israel's divine calling to possess the Promised Land.

When a person, a people group, or even an entire generation refuses to heed the call of God, God is not going to beg for obedience or for a willing heart. Instead, He will pass over that person or group of people and use someone else. The Lord has X-ray vision. He sees straight through a person and looks at their heart. When the Lord released tumultuous times, the Israelites repented. However, it was not genuine. We see this happen all the time today. People live how they want until there is a catastrophe or sudden death. All of a sudden, people begin to look to God. While this is wonderful that people are looking up, the devotion often doesn't last long.

Psalm 78:32-38 (NLT) says, "But in spite of this, the people kept sinning. Despite His wonders, they refused to trust Him. So He ended their lives in failure, their years in terror. When God began killing them, they finally sought Him. They repented and took God seriously. Then they remembered that God was their rock, that God Most High was their redeemer. But all they gave Him was lip service; they lied to Him with their tongues. Their hearts were not loyal to Him. They did not keep His covenant. Yet He was merciful and forgave their sins and did not destroy them all. Many times He held back His anger and did not unleash His fury!"

A person's heart is what God sees and values most. External acts and spoken words are secondary to what is in the heart. Hebrews 4:13 (NIV) tells us, "Nothing in all creation is hidden from God's sight. Everything is uncovered and laid bare before the eyes of Him to whom we must give account." A loyal, devoted heart is what leads to promotion from God. When the Israelites rebelled, God always had a leader whom He raised up. One of the greatest leaders in Israel's history that God lifted high was King David.

Psalm 78:70-72 (ESV) tells us, "He chose David His servant and took him from the sheepfolds; from following the nursing ewes He brought him to shepherd Jacob His people, Israel His inheritance. With upright heart he shepherded them and guided them with his skillful hand." If you have ever read much about David, you know that David was far from perfect in his lifetime. He committed adultery. He arranged to have the innocent killed (see 2 Samuel 11). He was arguably not a very good father (see 2 Samuel 13 for the drama between David's children Amnon, Tamar, and Absalom). His pride got the best of him at times (see 1 Chronicles 21).

The reason God chose David and blessed him despite his shortcomings, but was furious with the congregation in the wilderness, is that God knew David's heart. There was a massive difference between David's heart and the hearts of those who fell in the wilderness. One might argue the Israelites in the wilderness had it hard, so maybe that's why they rebelled. They just came out of slavery. It was hot in the wilderness. There was limited provision. They didn't know what they were doing.

However, David went through just as many trials - if not more - than his ancestors. David was hunted to be killed for much of his life. Those closest to him betrayed him (Psalm 41:9). He had a kingdom with threats from every side. His own son Absalom tried to overthrow him and take the throne. A life full of hardships did not deter David from finishing strong in his faith. The same is true for us. There is one thing all people on the planet are guaranteed: there are going to be many problems in life. Jesus made it clear that this world is full of trouble (John 16:33).

One reason the Israelites went through trial after trial in the wilderness is that God was intentionally testing them. He was using the hardship to show what was in their hearts. Deuteronomy 8:1-2 (NKJV) says, "Every commandment which I command you today you must be careful to observe, that you may live and multiply, and go in and possess the land of which the LORD swore to your fathers. And you shall remember that the LORD your God led you all the way these forty years in the wilderness, to humble you and test you, to know what was in your heart, whether you would keep His commandments or not."

Figuratively speaking, there is a special Promised Land for every believer in this life. There is a mission to fulfill, a destiny to reach, and a purpose to live out. This morning, I was brushing my teeth, and I heard the Lord say to me, "McKade, I have already laid out the plans for you since before I created the world." In other words, God already knows what He has planned for my future and has had planned for a very long time. As long as I stay close to Him, those plans are certainly going to be fulfilled. Shortly after I heard the Lord speak those words, I also heard the words, "Jeremiah 29:11".

The reason God spoke this to me is that I have a propensity to obsess over the future and to worry. I can grow a "to-do" list exponentially just by getting ready for bed every night. I worry about what my life will look like at age 85, and I'm not even halfway there yet! At times, I have to check myself and repent for worrying and obsessing. Jesus tells us not to worry (Philippians 4:6). When we worry, it's really a lack of faith we are dealing with. Faith knows that God already has all things planned and in order. While God does expect us to be responsible, address issues, and take serious matters seriously, He does not want us to try to fill His role for Him.

Psalm 78 was written so that we might know how important it is to remember all of the wonderful things God has done for us and to also remember not to be stubborn and unbelieving. Whenever we find ourselves violating what we know God has commanded us to do, we need to ask for forgiveness. We need to thank God for giving us another chance, a repeat, a do-over - praise Him for being merciful and kind, quick to forgive and ready to help us get back up.

The Lord did not abandon Israel in the wilderness after delivering them out of slavery. Instead, He used the children of the generation that rebelled. The same is true today. Even if an entire generation of people were to stop going to church, stop preaching, and stop standing for the Word of God in the culture, God would still raise up another generation to teach and preach His Word. Why? Because God is faithful. One generation's disobedience and stubbornness will never nullify God's promises.

Right now, the Lord has His hand stretched down from Heaven, calling on you to receive Him. God has a purpose and a special plan for you in this world. He knew you before you were ever born. Your identity and who you are can only be found in Him. God's desire has always been to have a relationship with you. Your reason for existence is to be in communion with Him. He wants to walk with you, talk with you, and let you experience His everlasting presence.

Spending time in the presence of the Lord is how you grow your relationship with Him. Abiding in His Word is where you are going to experience victory and freedom. Singing God's praises is what stirs up your faith to believe for signs, wonders, and miracles. You are never more powerful than when you are in the secret place with your Father. It's how David defeated powerful armies against all odds. It's how Jesus defeated the enemy on the Cross and overcame this world. It's how the Apostle Paul grew to become the greatest leader of the early church.

Your strength does not come from people or money. Your strength comes from the Lord. Zechariah 4:6 (ESV) reminds us, "Not by might, nor by power, but by My Spirit, says the LORD of hosts." The prophet Jeremiah declares in Jeremiah 9:23-24 (NASB95), "Thus says the LORD, 'Let not a wise man boast of his wisdom, and let not the mighty man boast of his might, let not a rich man boast of his riches; but let him who boasts boast of this, that he understands and knows Me, that I am the LORD who exercises lovingkindness, justice and righteousness on earth; for I delight in these things,' declares the LORD."

God is breaking barriers and knocking down doors in your life. Your faith is what's defeating the enemy. Because you believe, all things are possible (Mark 9:23). The Lord is your front and rear guard (Isaiah 52:12). You are leaving behind the old ways of thinking and stepping into the new things God has in store for you. Your steps are ordered by the Lord (Psalm 37:23). Your ears are open to hear what God is speaking directly to your heart.

As you stay devoted to the Lord, you are rising higher. You are overcoming obstacles. You are finding success. If God can create the entire world in six days, then imagine what He can do in your life when you place your trust in Him. The Lord is enlarging your faith to believe bigger, aim higher, and go further than you ever thought possible. Your trials are becoming your triumphs. Your tests are becoming your testimonies. You are going to new levels of victory like never before in Jesus' name.

SCRIPTURE READING

Deuteronomy 8:1-5

Psalm 78:1-7

Luke 16:25-31

Philippians 4:6-7

QUESTIONS TO ANSWER

Have you ever gone through a period of rebellion in your life? What kept you from receiving God's love and from following Him? *(In other words, what was holding you back?)*

Do you believe God already planned everything about your entire life before He created the world? If so, what causes you to worry about your future?

Where is your favorite place to go where you can feel God's presence? *(For example: the park, outdoors in nature, a favorite recliner, a church, etc.)*

Chapter Nineteen
STAYING IN FAITH

A lifestyle of faith always has been and always will be very personal. Who a person is or is perceived to be while in public, or even around loved ones and those they are closest to, is still only surface-level compared to what a person truly believes deep down. Even people we see at church each week may not have the exact same beliefs as us. The depths of one's heart is something only God sees. The external religious acts of a man are just that: external. What's on the inside is of far greater value.

For centuries, arguments have arisen from within the churches over various doctrines and ways of doing church. The ideologies of different men and women of faith have birthed all sorts of churches and denominations around the world. While diversity within the church is a blessing, the petty arguments and divisions are not. The Apostle Paul tells the church in Romans 16:17 (NIV), "I urge you, brothers and sisters, to watch out for those who cause divisions and put obstacles in your way that are contrary to the teaching you have learned. Keep away from them."

People who go around causing division and stirring others up against one another are not of God. The Scriptures call these people busybodies and meddlers. 1 Timothy 5:13 (BSB) says, "At the same time they will also learn to be idle, going from house to house and being not only idle, but also gossips and busybodies, discussing things they should not mention."

God has called all believers to work and have a diligent hand. There is always work to do if you are serving the Lord. Retirement does not come until you are six feet under, or the trumpet blasts to meet Jesus in the air. We are required to live a life of faith. This means we move forward by trusting God, His Word, and His Spirit to lead us to the next thing He may have for us to do.

I always marvel at how quickly (especially in the western world) people want to "retire" - make so much money sooner than expected so that we can "retire" at a younger age. We want to "get rich" so we can "retire" and never work again. If you are following Jesus Christ, you never get to retire. John 5:17 (NIV) says, "In His defense Jesus said to them, 'My Father is always at His work to this very day, and I too am working.'" God the Father is always working. Is there poverty in the world? Yep. Then the Father is still working to help those who are starving, and He expects you to be a part of that plan.

Is there crime and violence in the world? You better believe it. Someone called by God has to bring justice. Are there spiritually lost people in your community? Somebody has to witness to them. There is work to do everywhere you turn. For anyone to say they are "retired" is almost a joke in light of eternity and the amount of God's work that needs to be done. Even the elderly have a place to work in God's Kingdom. Some of the greatest intercessors and those who can impart great wisdom can only be found among the elderly.

The Apostle Paul tells us in Romans 14:22-23 (NIV), "So whatever you believe about these things keep between yourself and God. Blessed is the one who does not condemn himself by what he approves. But whoever has doubts is condemned if they eat, because their eating is not from faith; and everything that does not come from faith is sin." When Paul said this, he was talking about cultural issues having to do primarily with food. Staying in faith for the sake of a good conscience before God is Paul's message in this passage.

Paul drives home the point of taking care of our freedom in Christ by not hurting others who are weak in their faith. Meat was sacrificed to idols in Paul's day, so some believers felt it was sin to eat the meat being sacrificed. However, Paul knew there was no such thing as a true idol, that there is only one God (1 Corinthians 8:4), so the meat in and of itself is not unclean or unholy when eaten in thanksgiving to God. He says in 1 Corinthians 8:13 (NIV), "Therefore, if what I eat causes my brother or sister to fall into sin, I will never eat meat again, so that I will not cause them to fall."

Some issues in this world aren't necessarily right or wrong. It's a principle of conscience and how things are perceived by those trying to walk out their faith in Jesus Christ. Spiritually speaking, we are already living in Babylon, so the secular world that doesn't follow Christ is now everywhere we go. The more we mature in Christ, the more we learn how to adapt and love others in the faith. A couple of years ago, there was some conflict brought up about something similar to what Paul was talking about regarding food and drink. A lot of Christians were upset with different businesses and refused to patronize their stores.

I knew why people had a problem with these specific stores, and I didn't necessarily disagree with them. However, I knew food was food, drinks were drinks, clothing was clothing, and some of these businesses employed people who were innocent and just trying to make a living. Instead of rubbing it in that I was "free in Christ" to eat what I want, drink what I want, and wear what I want, I became more sensitive to the matter. I didn't raise my voice or take a public stand saying this side or that side was wrong. Instead, I stuck to what God had called me to do in that season. I worked. I wrote. I ministered and taught at the church.

This being said, there are certain things that are black and white based on God's Word. That's not what I am talking about. God has given every person a conscience to tell them what is right and what is wrong. He has given His Word to instruct us and show us the way to live. When a person begins to reject their conscience and reject God's Word, the Bible says their conscience becomes "seared like a hot iron" (1 Timothy 4:2). Their senses to feel remorse for sin and wrongdoing are dulled and even eliminated. Because the culture has drifted so far from God, not just in America but around the world, there is a moral numbness that has set in.

As believers, we are called to stay in faith while living in a culture that does not honor God. Staying in faith means we stay devoted to reading the Bible. It means we keep our hearts turned towards God as we go through life's battles. It means we reject fear when we could dwell on worrisome thoughts and potential problems that lie ahead. The way we defeat fear is by staying in faith. For example, when I am traveling, I have to remind myself that God has already gone before me. Traveling can be both exciting and stressful. There are itineraries to adhere to, making sure things are in order at home before leaving, attending to bills before and after the trip, and a long list of to-dos around travel time.

I remember one time I was waiting for my luggage after a flight, and I started to get frantic. The fearful thoughts began to run rampant: "What if my bags were sent with the wrong flight? My medicine is in that specific bag. My favorite shoes are in there. How long until I find the bag? What if they can't find it?" All of a sudden, something rose up in me. It was my faith. I found myself uttering under my breath, "Stay in faith, McKade." As I began to reassure myself that God had everything under control, a peace started to set in. I kept hearing God's voice in me, telling me to stay in faith. Shortly thereafter, the baggage carousel turned on and began to spin. As I waited, the bags began to roll out.

Sure enough, after several bags passed by, there were my bags. Nothing was lost. I remember this experience at the airport vividly because I remember the fear that came over me that evening while waiting for my luggage. A lesson was learned that night.

Staying in faith isn't just something I've had to learn to do at an airport; it's a practice I've had to learn through any situation I face from day to day. It's learning to not just plan and prepare, to try and do my best, but to trust the omnipotent power of God in my life.

God promises us in Deuteronomy 31:8 (BSB), "The LORD Himself goes before you; He will be with you. He will never leave you nor forsake you. Do not be afraid or discouraged." Isaiah 52:12 (NIV) tells us, "But you will not leave in haste or go in flight; for the LORD will go before you, the God of Israel will be your rear guard." Knowing that God is ahead of us and behind us should give us confidence that we can trust Him during any battle we are facing. There is a victory ahead. We just have to keep pressing forward in faith, knowing God and His holy angels are warring against the enemy on our behalf.

When I played football in junior high and high school, I was one of the primary running backs. This means I was responsible for taking the football from the quarterback's hand and attempting to run as far as I could ahead until I eventually reached the end zone to score a touchdown. As the running back, I had an entire line of guys in front of me whose goal was to block the opponent so I would have room to run down the field and score. Furthermore, when I had the ball, the entire team would do all they could to protect me from being tackled. That meant that as I ran, my teammates would block anyone in front of me and anyone chasing me trying to put a stop to me scoring. I had to have faith in my teammates to give their all to defend me, and they had to have faith in me that I ran as hard as I could to try and score for the team.

In the same way, in the unseen spiritual realm, God has angels and His Spirit blocking and blinding the enemy. We have the same goal. The opponent is the devil and his horde of demons. We must trust the power of the Lord, and His angelic armies are moving on our behalf. When we believe, there is a supernatural power released. The internal battle between faith and fear is part of being human. When Jesus walked on water, He never sank because He walked in perfect faith. He did the impossible effortlessly. He knew who He was. Jesus never had an identity crisis. He knew He was the Son of God.

We see faith rise up, then fear overtakes faith, when the disciple Peter musters up enough courage to join Jesus on the raging sea (see Matthew 14:25-33). At first, Peter's faith in Christ was so strong that he stood on water. However, as Peter looked around at what was happening, his logic kicked in. He saw the crashing waves. He realized he was walking on water and should be sinking. Because of his own understanding of the laws of nature, his faith became weak. Instead of walking all the way to Jesus, Peter began to sink. The lesson from Peter's doubt is that logic and faith rarely agree.

Human logic has hindered man's faith since the beginning of time. Greatness starts by first believing a dream can be achieved. Believing before seeing is faith. Before there was an airplane in existence, someone had to believe that it was possible to build an aircraft that could transport a person via flying high in the sky. The Wright brothers achieved the seemingly impossible in 1903 when they built the first-ever aircraft, the Wright Flyer. It took the brothers, Orville and Wilbur Wright, half a decade of intense study and research before they successfully built a flying mode of transportation that would revolutionize the world.

Today, generations later, we experience the blessings of those who worked hard and believed the impossible could be achieved. If it weren't for the faith of our ancestors, we would not have many of the modern conveniences and technologies we mindlessly enjoy. Without discoveries made in how electricity works, we would not have light switches, air conditioners, or anything powered by the electrical grid in our homes and businesses. We have Thomas Edison (and other brilliant minds) to thank. Without generational blessings, the world would be in much worse shape.

On the flip side, there are still generational curses that have plagued the world for millennia. There have been zero years without armed conflict for centuries. The wars and rumors of wars Jesus foretold are still playing out (Matthew 24:6). With every great revolution or spiritual revival, there has also been turmoil, persecution, and loss of life. Some of the biggest genocides in history have occurred in the last one hundred years. Almost one million lives were lost in the Rwanda Genocide of 1994. More than six million Jews and others were systemically rounded up and killed in the Holocaust (1939-1945). Joseph Stalin (1929-1953) and Mao Zedong (1949-1976) murdered millions under their regimes.

There have been periods in history where faith broke forth like the rising sun, and there have been times where darkness seemed to have overtaken the world like the dead of night. Through it all, God's faithfulness always prevailed. His Word has withstood the test of time. When we read what the Lord's prophets have spoken in the Scriptures, we see that their words are still living and active, always at work. What was spoken to Israel and God's people years ago is meant for us too.

Psalm 33:9 (NASB) tells us, "For He spoke, and it was done; He commanded, and it stood firm." Right now, God is speaking over you. He is speaking words of life and victory. He is speaking, "It is done." (John 19:30) When Jesus died on the Cross, He defeated the enemy for all of us. We already have victory because of Christ's sacrifice. The promises of God to you throughout the Scriptures are "yes and amen" in Jesus' name (2 Corinthians 1:20). Staying in faith means we agree with these promises, regardless of what the secular world is saying. When we say, "Amen," we are saying, "I agree."

Without a vision, the people perish (Proverbs 29:18). The word of the Lord has been given so that we will have a sense of purpose, direction, and divine freedom that comes from Heaven. You were born for such a time as this (Esther 4:14). Whether you are in

Generation Beta (2025-2039), Generation Alpha (2010-2024), Generation Z (1997-2010), the Millennial Generation (1981-1996), Generation X (1965-1980), the Baby Boom Generation (1946-1964), the Silent Generation (1928-1945), or the Greatest Generation (1901-1927), you were ordained by God to come into this world at just the right time.

Your birth year is not happenstance. How do I know this? God told us so. Ephesians 2:10 (NLT) says, "For we are God's masterpiece. He has created us anew in Christ Jesus, so we can do the good things He planned for us long ago." I don't know how many years "long ago" is in God's eyes, but I believe it was long before time ever began. Our destiny was prepared in the eternal realm where God dwells. Ephesians 1:4 (NLT) tells us, "Even before He made the world, God loved us and chose us in Christ to be holy and without fault in His eyes." Before Adam and Eve, before He said, "Let there be light," God already knew you would be a "Baby Boomer" or a "Millennial" (or whatever generation you are in).

God is causing His plans for your life to come together. Ephesians 1:11 (NLT) says, "Furthermore, because we are united with Christ, we have received an inheritance from God, for He chose us in advance, and He makes everything work out according to His plan." God's plans are always good. Your family, your job, your finances, your strengths, your struggles, your health, and all things pertaining to your life are in the hands of your Creator. He is omnipotent, not semi-omnipotent. He is in full control, not partial supremacy. There is nothing outside of His reach and no situation too difficult for Him to change.

The eyes of the Lord are everywhere at all times (Proverbs 15:3). He knows what's going on, whether good or evil. When we make decisions based on our faith and convictions, no one else may see but God does, and God is a rewarder of those who do what is right and operate in faith (Hebrews 11:6). Staying in faith doesn't mean we ignore problems. It means we rise above them. Staying in faith doesn't mean we never struggle. It means we overcome by trusting in our Savior, Jesus.

You are going to leave your mark on this generation as you follow Jesus Christ. You are a massive salt block of faith in this world (Matthew 5:13). God is using you to season people in their faith, bring shalom peace to those you encounter, and preserve the faith in your family line. Your devotion to the Lord is noticed not just by the Lord but by those around you. Even when you don't see change yet, God is still causing all things to work together for the good.

SCRIPTURE READING

Deuteronomy 31:6-9

Isaiah 52:12-15

Romans 14:17-23

Ephesians 1:9-14

QUESTIONS TO ANSWER

When is a time, or a stressful situation, in which you had to "stay in faith" instead of fear?

How did you overcome the trial or the difficulty? *(For example: by praying, holding to a Scripture, keeping yourself busy with work, etc.)*

What are the characteristics of the generation you were born in *(like Gen X, Gen Z, etc)*? What attributes do you share with your specific generation? What about those attributes are good? Those that are bad? How can you align your generation's values with God's values found in His Word?

Chapter Twenty
LEAVING A LEGACY

Leaving a legacy of faith is the highest mark of a true believer when they depart from this world. Our legacy is all that remains after we die. Our values, character, actions, and memories with others are what connect one generation to another. In my family line, there is a strong legacy of the cowboy way. My grandparents and great-grandparents wore cowboy hats, walked around in boots, carried around a Bible, and took life by the horns with a hard work ethic. The legacy of my ancestors has made a lasting impression on my family and me.

There is only one thing that is guaranteed in life. The only guarantee is death (unless we are the one fortunate generation that is taken in the rapture). While none of us know when our time is up, we are taught by the Scriptures to prepare for the future, even after we are gone. Proverbs 13:22 (NASB) says, "A good person leaves an inheritance to his grandchildren, and the wealth of a sinner is stored up for the righteous." The inheritance you leave can be material assets like money, property, or businesses. It can be non-material blessings like faith, Christian values, wisdom, or a hard work ethic.

A good legacy provides benefits to future generations and gives a foundation for their success. How we build a legacy requires wisdom. Psalm 90:12 (NIV) tells us, "Teach us to number our days, that we may gain a heart of wisdom." Legacy planning is the best thing you can do for you and your loved ones before you pass away. Beyond writing a legal will, make amends with anyone God puts on your heart so you won't go to the grave full of regret. Right before my mom passed away, I didn't know that it would be on my fortieth birthday that I would talk to her for the last time on the phone while standing on the beach in Malibu. Twenty days later, I would never be able to speak with her again.

The day she passed away, it was the most painful experience I have ever been through in my life. A giant hole was blasted through my soul. Only the grace of God has helped me live with it. Her legacy was believing her children could do anything. She was a cheerleader, inside and out. She never told me I wasn't good enough or didn't have what it takes. When I played basketball, she believed I was going to be in the NBA. When I wrote a book, she believed it would be the best seller. Her faith in her children was indisputable. To this day, I believe I can do anything. That belief is in large part due to my parents always telling me I could do anything I set my mind to achieve.

They weren't wrong. I have excelled far beyond what I could ever imagine. I've obtained college degrees, written five books, traveled overseas (Israel included), and written a screenplay that is now being prepared for the Hollywood big screen. Having parents who spoke life into me, especially in my weakest moments, is the best gift they could have ever given me. Likewise, your legacy doesn't have to be some complex, drawn-out plan. Your legacy can be believing your children and grandchildren are going to become all God created them to be.

Your legacy is much greater than a trust fund or legal will. Your legacy is what you speak into your loved ones while you are still alive. In the New Testament, the Apostle Paul commends Timothy for walking in the legacy of faith imparted to him by his grandmother and his mother. Paul says in 2 Timothy 1:5 (NLT), "I remember your genuine faith, for you share the faith that first filled your grandmother Lois and your mother, Eunice. And I know that same faith continues strong in you." Leaving a legacy of faith like Grandmother Lois and Mother Eunice is what makes for tremendous followers of Jesus Christ, like Paul's fellow worker Timothy.

The Apostle Paul goes on to tell Timothy, "Therefore I remind you to stir up the gift of God which is in you through the laying on of my hands. For God has not given us a spirit of fear, but of power and of love and of a sound mind." (2 Timothy 1:6-7 NKJV) Your legacy can be breaking powerful generational yokes that have created barriers in your family line for generations. Laying your hands on those you love to pray can release blessings that will overtake your family for many years to come. Hereditary diseases, mental illness, poverty, lack of education, and any other shortcomings or deficiencies that have seemed to have plagued your family can come to an end in Jesus' name.

Your prayers and your walk with God can transform lives long after you are gone. The greatest example of a legacy that lasts is none other than Jesus, the Son of God. Jesus' biggest impact on the world wasn't while He was alive. Conversely, it was only after His death that the world would be revolutionized. He tells the disciples in John 12:23-24 (NIV), "The hour has come for the Son of Man to be glorified. Very truly I tell you, unless a kernel of wheat falls to the ground and dies, it remains only a single seed. But if it dies, it produces many seeds." Again, He says in John 16:7 (NASB), "But I tell you the truth: it is to your advantage that I am leaving; for if I do not leave, the Helper will not come to you; but if I go, I will send Him to you."

The Holy Spirit is the promise fulfilled from Jesus' death on the cross and resurrection from the dead. Because Jesus sent the Holy Spirit just as He promised He would, we now have God's presence living and abiding in our hearts. This holy indwelling is what sets us apart from the world. Christ's Spirit is the seed of promise God spoke about to our father Abraham (Genesis 22:18, Galatians 3:16). You carry this seed with you everywhere you go. Scattering God's seed is what you do for an eternal legacy. Be sure to share the seed of God's Kingdom with everyone you can!

Jesus says in Matthew 6:20-21 (NLT), "Store your treasures in heaven, where moths and rust cannot destroy, and thieves do not break in and steal. Wherever your treasure is, there the desires of your heart will also be." God's heavenly kingdom is the seed you can plant into anyone you meet. It's the living seed that ensures you will see your loved ones in Heaven when they receive Jesus into their hearts. Sharing Bible verses, taking people to church, and singing God's praises are how you spread the seed of Christ's Spirit all around.

Another way to ensure an eternal legacy is to use your financial resources to advance God's kingdom. The Apostle Paul tells Timothy in 1 Timothy 6:18-19 (NLT), "Tell them [the rich] to use their money to do good. They should be rich in good works and generous to those in need, always being ready to share with others. By doing this they will be storing up their treasure as a good foundation for the future so that they may experience true life." Helping provide and meet the needs of others when you are able to is at the center of God's heart. God's heart is to help the sick, needy, weak, and less fortunate.

One of the most life-changing trips I ever made was a mission trip to Mozambique, Africa. Mozambique is one of the poorest countries in the world. While at a Zimpeto orphanage in the nation's capital, Maputo, I witnessed extreme poverty firsthand. There were trash dumps alongside the road that were higher than NBA basketball backboards. Many of the children didn't even know who their parents were or where their next meal might come from, especially if they ever left the orphanage. However, they were some of the happiest kids in the world.

They loved hanging out with all the missionaries and playing sports. One of the most touching moments I had with three of the children was when we went to visit a "convenience" store nearby. Granted, the store was rather barren and unstocked, but there was enough merchandise for each of us to grab a chocolate bar and a bottle of soda. I pulled out some meticais (Mozambican currency) to pay for the treats, and we headed back to the orphanage down the road. When we arrived back safely, one of the kids gave his candy bar to his younger brother. As I watched, my eyes watered. Here was a child who had so little, and yet he was so selfless to give away a rare treat.

While there have been many from First World countries who have visited these orphanages, some of the universal lessons learned by us all are the same. Those here who are materially poor are some of the happiest, most faith-filled people in the world. They live in an alternate reality from most of us. At first, most of us feel compassion, and even pity, for these poor Mozambicans. However, the feelings ironically reverse when we realize how rich and gluttonous we are by comparison. Sure, here in the United States and other developed countries, we have cars, houses, education, and any kind of food or beverage the heart desires, but we lack much of what these materially poor people possess.

These people I met weren't on a time crunch. They weren't perpetually stressed, constantly checking their watches and smartphones, all wrought up about when the next meeting was. They weren't pulling their hair out and constantly fighting. Instead, they were grateful and enjoyed even the smallest things in life. The moral of the story: true life is upside down from what the world defines as life. God's kingdom is upside down from the patterns of this world. We are taught that more money, a higher income, a bigger house, and fame are what matter most, and yet, most of us find ourselves miserable as we pursue these material things. The Apostle James tells in James 2:5 (NIV), "Listen, my dear brothers and sisters: Has not God chosen those who are poor in the eyes of the world to be rich in faith and to inherit the kingdom He promised those who love Him?"

The laws of nature in God's kingdom teach us that the poor are naturally richer in faith.

One reason for this is that people who have material wealth tend to place their faith in what their money and influence can do instead of what God can do. The poor often cannot defend themselves using worldly means like the wealthy can. Proverbs 31:8-9 (NIV) says, "Speak up for those who cannot speak for themselves, for the rights of all who are destitute. Speak up and judge fairly; defend the rights of the poor and needy." When you speak out to defend the innocent, you are fulfilling your divine calling. You are making a difference that will impact lives, even after you are gone. You are leaving a legacy.

When I think of a missionary who left a lasting legacy after her death, I think of Mother Teresa. Mother Teresa was a Catholic nun and saint who took care of the poorest of the poor. She built homes for orphans, nursing homes, and hospices for the terminally ill in India. She is known for saying, "Do small things with great love." In other words, it's not just grandiose giving or monumental deeds that change the world. It's the small acts of love and kindness in everyday life that can make a big difference. Not everyone can build an orphanage or be a missionary overseas full-time, but anyone can show an act of love and kindness towards another right where they are.

Your legacy is made by the decisions you make on a daily basis. When you choose to honor God, you are building a legacy. When you wake up in the morning and spend time with the Lord, you are building your faith to do the Father's work that is going to last forever. When Moses commissions Joshua and the Israelites to take their God-ordained promised land, He tells them in Deuteronomy 30:19-20 (BSB), "I call heaven and earth as witnesses against you today that I have set before you life and death, blessing and cursing. Therefore choose life, so that you and your descendants may live, and that you may love the LORD your God, obey Him, and hold fast to Him. For He is your life, and He will prolong your life in the land that the LORD swore to give to your fathers, to Abraham, Isaac, and Jacob."

Your descendants, those who come after you, are going to be impacted by the decisions you make while still alive. Generational blessings are released simply because you are choosing to follow God and honor His Word. Your devotion to Him is the greatest legacy you can leave for the next generation. God is always speaking to each generation if they will only listen. The royal psalm tells us, "For the LORD is good. His unfailing love continues forever, and His faithfulness continues to each generation." (Psalm 100:5 NLT) From Adam and Eve in the Garden of Eden until the end of time, God always has been and always will be an ever-present help in times of trouble to every single generation (Psalm 46:1).

The Apostle Paul summarizes it best on Mars Hill when he tells the men of Athens in Acts 17:24-28 (BSB), "The God who made the world and everything in it is the Lord of heaven and earth and does not live in temples made by human hands. Nor is He served by human hands, as if He needed anything, because He Himself gives everyone life and breath and everything else. From one man He made every nation of men, that they should inhabit the whole earth; and He determined their appointed times and the boundaries of their lands. God intended that they would seek Him and perhaps reach out for Him and find Him, though He is not far from each one of us. 'For in Him we live and move and have our being.' As some of your own poets have said, 'We are His offspring.'"

We are all God's children in that we are made in His image. However, only those who come to Him in Jesus' name are part of the eternal inheritance. We must come to Jesus for forgiveness of sins to be made right before our Maker. No one is exempt. The Scriptures warn us, "Let no one deceive you with empty words, for because of such things the wrath of God is coming on the sons of disobedience." (Ephesians 5:6 BSB) There are two types of people in this world, and both types are God's children. There are the children of "obedience" and the children of "disobedience".

The first type of person is the one who accepts the gospel, Christ's free gift of salvation, and is forgiven and made right in God's eyes. The other type of person is the one who hears the gospel but rejects it. Because they don't put their faith in Jesus, there is no forgiveness of sins. Without forgiveness, no one can enter Heaven because everyone has sin in their life (Romans 3:23). No one is in Heaven that isn't supposed to be there, and no one is in Hell who isn't supposed to be there. God tells us He already knew who would accept Him and who would reject Him. He knows all who belong to Him (2 Timothy 2:19).

The good news is that the moment you confess and believe in Jesus, you are saved (Romans 10:9). Your faith in Christ is what saves you for all eternity. In Christ, you have an eternal legacy that will last forever and ever. The last chapter of the Bible tells you about your final destination. Your final destination is to reign with Christ forever. Revelation 22:3-5 (NLT) says, "No longer will there be a curse upon anything. For the throne of God and of the Lamb will be there, and His servants will worship Him. And they will see His face, and His name will be written on their foreheads. And there will be no night there—no need for lamps or sun—for the Lord God will shine on them. And they will reign forever and ever."

Your final destination is full of peace and life like you've never seen or experienced before. The prophet Isaiah tells us, "The wolf will live with the lamb, and the leopard will lie down with the goat; the calf and young lion and fatling will be together, and a little child will lead them. The cow will graze with the bear, their young will lie down together, and the lion will eat straw like the ox. The infant will play by the cobra's den, and the toddler will reach into the viper's nest. They will neither harm nor destroy on all My holy mountain, for the earth will be full of the knowledge of the LORD as the sea is full of water. On that day the Root of Jesse [Jesus] will stand as a banner for the peoples. The nations will seek Him, and His place of rest will be glorious." (Isaiah 11:6-10 BSB)

What you leave behind will testify to the high calling of God on your life (Philippians 3:14). Your faith will be remembered when God calls you to come home. One day, a minister will conduct your funeral, sharing your life and deeds with friends, family, and loved ones. People will tell jokes of "remember that time when...". The minister will recount how you chose to live your life for the Lord. Those who know God will grieve, but they will have peace knowing you are in Heaven with Jesus (1 Thessalonians 4:13).

You are going to be remembered for your charity and good deeds. Your legacy is going to be how you loved the ones God placed in your life while you were still alive. Your legacy of faith and love is going to pass from one generation to the next. The devotion you have will be reflected in the lives of those who are to follow. Right after your last breath, you will go from having only glimpses of God's glory and presence here to a permanent, full view of God's glory for all eternity.

SCRIPTURE READING

Proverbs 13:19-25

Isaiah 11:6-10

Philippians 3:12-16

2 Timothy 1:3-9

QUESTIONS TO ANSWER

What do you want your legacy to be when you pass away?

How can you prepare now to leave that legacy for the generations to come?

If you died today, would you be ready to meet Jesus? Do you know with certainty where you would spend eternity? If not, now is the time to ask Jesus into your heart. Ask Him to forgive you of all your sins and make Him your personal Lord and Savior.

CONCLUSION

As you look ahead to what comes next, remember God has already gone before you. When Jesus was headed to the Cross, He already knew the victory that was coming after the necessary suffering on Calvary. The Scriptures say in Hebrews 12:2-3 (BSB), "Let us fix our eyes on Jesus, the author and perfecter of our faith, who for the joy set before Him endured the cross, scorning its shame, and sat down at the right hand of the throne of God. Consider Him who endured such hostility from sinners, so that you will not grow weary and lose heart." Jesus took on sin, death, and the grave with deep, immovable joy because He knew the outcome.

Jesus knew He would inherit you. He knew His act on the Cross as the Son of God would be the bridge between Heaven and earth. He knew He would be seated at the right hand of the Father to rule and reign for eternity as Mediator and King. The depths of heartache and pain Jesus went through for us are unimaginable. While fleeing Jerusalem during his own son Absalom's rebellion, King David declared, "Deep calls to deep in the roar of Your waterfalls; all Your breakers and waves have rolled over me. The LORD decrees His loving devotion by day, and at night His song is with me as a prayer to the God of my life." (Psalm 42:7-8 BSB)

The deep sufferings of Christ opened the door to deep riches from the Father for all mankind. As we go deep in knowing how much we need God, His love is going to go even deeper. At the bottom of the ocean, there are lost treasures. There are mysteries at this depth level that are hidden from the eyes of the world. In the same way, God has preserved deep treasures He longs to reveal to you as you abide in His presence. Jesus tells us that He discloses Himself only to those who love Him and are seeking Him (John 14:21). King Solomon tells us that it is God's glory to keep matters hidden, and it is royalty's glory to search out the matter (Proverbs 25:2).

The more you seek out the things of God and His Kingdom, the more you are going to discover riches that are far beyond what this world can see. Covenants are formed in the deep places of your heart when you draw close to the Lord. Generational blessings are stored up in ways far beyond what you can imagine. The Word of God tells us in Deuteronomy 7:9 (NLT), "Understand, therefore, that the LORD your God is indeed God. He is the faithful God who keeps His covenant for a thousand generations and lavishes His unfailing love on those who love Him and obey His commands."

A thousand generations… In other words, His covenant is endless. His love is consistent and never fails for generations to come. His blessings for you and your loved ones are boundless. The only thing that holds back more of God's favor in your life is a lack of faith. Unbelief is what can turn off the spigot of God's favor. Paul warns us in Romans 11:20 (BSB), "That is correct: They were broken off because of unbelief, but you stand by faith. Do not be arrogant, but be afraid."

A humble heart and a willing spirit are what please the Lord. Believing God will do what He says He will do is what brings His favor. Hebrews 11:1-3 (BSB) says, "Now faith is the assurance of what we hope for and the certainty of what we do not see. This is why the ancients were commended. By faith we understand that the universe was formed at God's command, so that what is seen was not made out of what was visible." God has been weaving His story through all generations.

With each generation, God instills greatness in His people. From the beginning, there has been the existence of darkness and evil. God's answer has always been and always will be to use people who are willing to put their trust in Him. We are His stars. Philippians 2:13-15 (NIV) tells us, "For it is God who works in you to will and to act in order to fulfill His good purpose. Do everything without grumbling or arguing, so that you may become blameless and pure, 'children of God without fault in a warped and crooked generation.' Then you will shine among them like stars in the sky."

The problems of this world are what actually make people like you and me shine. When we keep doing our best to live for God, reading the Bible, praying, and encouraging one another, we are shining. When we mess up, we get back up. We ask the Father to forgive us, and we keep moving forward. The Hebrew word for "move forward" is kadima. Through all of life's battles, we must kadima. We must continue to charge onward in faith.

The way we gain ground, see success, and experience revival is by carrying God's Word like a sword. His Word is what slices the enemy's plans up. His Word is what the angels honor when they go to work. His Word is eternal and never fails. For any area of life in which I struggle, I have a Bible verse to combat that struggle. When I feel impoverished, like I'll never have enough resources to do what is in my heart, I quote the Scriptures: "And my God shall supply all your need according to His riches in glory by Christ Jesus." (Philippians 4:19 NKJV)

When I find myself in messy situations that have no resolution in sight but can only get worse, I remember God's promise: "And we know that all things work together for good to those who love God, to those who are the called according to His purpose." (Romans 8:28 NKJV) When I'm fighting a health problem or feeling deathly ill, I remind myself and the enemy of what God says: "He forgives all my sins and heals all my diseases." (Psalm 103:3 NLT) I have seen God show up and deliver me through troubles time and time again.

God has a purpose for every living soul. Finding out that purpose is a lifelong journey. It's going through some things that change your character and your heart. It's experiencing God in real life. The good news is God never leaves us, no matter how fierce or overwhelming our battles may seem. In conclusion, I leave you with this verse to remind you that no matter how bad things get on earth, God is always there:

"When you go through deep waters, I will be with you. When you go through rivers of difficulty, you will not drown. When you walk through the fire of oppression, you will not be burned up; the flames will not consume you." Isaiah 43:2 (NLT)

www.ingramcontent.com/pod-product-compliance
Lightning Source LLC
Chambersburg PA
CBHW070951180426
43194CB00042B/2246